PERMISSION TO NARRATE

PERMISSION TO NARRATE
Explorations in Group Analysis, Psychoanalysis, Culture

Martin Weegmann

KARNAC

First published in 2016 by
Karnac Books Ltd
118 Finchley Road
London NW3 5HT

British Library Cataloguing in Publication Data

A C.I.P. for this book is available from the British Library

ISBN-13: 978-1-78220-362-9

Typeset by V Publishing Solutions Pvt Ltd., Chennai, India

Printed in Great Britain by TJ International Ltd, Padstow, Cornwall

www.karnacbooks.com

To Daniel and Mark, for everything, always . . . .

CONTENTS

ACKNOWLEDGEMENTS

For their encouragement and feedback, my heartfelt thanks to:

Rachel Cohen, Liesel Hearst, Hubert Hermans, Edward Khantzian, Morris Nitsun, Malcolm Pines, Alistair Sweet, David Winter, and to members of the "Readers and Writers Group" (2015)—Jale Cilasun, Monica Doran, Ryan Kemp, Lawrence Ladden, Kevin Power.

Appreciation to the Wellcome Library, London, for its incredible world of learning.

ABOUT THE AUTHOR

Martin Weegmann is a consultant clinical psychologist and group analyst, who is a specialist in substance misuse and personality disorders and is a well-known trainer. Martin edited *Psychodynamics of Addiction* (2002, Wiley) and *Group Psychotherapy and Addiction* (2004, Wiley), and has published many book chapters and papers in a range of journals. His book *The World Within the Group: Developing Theory for Group Analysis* (Karnac, 2014) is a major contribution to group analysis. He is working on a new edited book, *Psychodynamics of Writing* (Karnac). Over time, his interests have broadened to include those connected to narration, rhetoric, and the "literary mind".

FOREWORD

Some of us by temperament and preference are more comfortable with narrative explanations about our surroundings and life than we are with empirical ones. In reading Martin Weegmann's book it's safe to conclude that I share with him the same overall inclination. A long time ago, when first venturing into the realm of writing and author-ship, in a context of seemingly light-hearted exchange, a colleague quipped that before thinking about writing one has to have something to write about. Indeed it is true and a truism, but beyond that, one has to develop the capacity to write well, effectively, and, as I think Martin Weegmann would add, "persuasively". Martin has mastered all of these, especially the last. He is persuasive because he is widely read in so many domains—classical, literary, humanities, and the clinical. But his mastery of writing goes beyond that. His thoughts and words are consistently evocative and compelling. I would anticipate that the reader will be enchanted and interested with his rich metaphors and turn of thoughts as he pursues matters that touch his and our humanity.

Martin Weegmann, in initiating his treatise on seeking "permission to narrate", provides an erudite primer on theories of rhetoric and its application to the multiple and varied ways we speak and communicate with each other. His gifts with words and as a writer immediately shine as he applies this frame to groups and how the narrative approaches they adopt can be ineffectual or can rise to a richer level of discourse. Weegmann prompts us on the distinction between Aristotle's perspective on rhetoric and that of Plato, the latter cynically stressing the use of words to mislead, versus Aristotle's defence of its importance involving persuasion, for example, in law and politics. Here in the United States, at the time of one more cycle of bitter and nasty exchange that our system of elections generates, Weegmann drawing on bygone eras of reason and enlightenment, reminds us that words and reasoning can rise to effective and meaningful persuasion or degenerate into debasement and pernicious attack. During the Medieval and Renaissance periods, Weegmann continues, the debate was revived whether rhetoric was the "noble art" as scholars of the time advanced, or, as Locke argued, rhetoric was an artificial use of words employed to deceive. He artfully explores this debate about rhetoric over centuries of intellectual discourse, including, for example, the early emphasis of the Quakers on "plain speech" and a patient silence, and in more recent time, the perspective of social scientist on the role of metaphor and "finding voice" as empowering and enriching; on the other hand, he refers to how speech and language can be used to hurt and hate.

Weegmann offers a lively example of a detox ward group therapy where there is initial resistance, wit, humour, and playfulness, but then there is a shift and the group spontaneously develops its own group context for serious exchange and meaningful discourse. As Martin wisely describes it, the group interaction is a sober new way of finding self with others. From his perspective, he calls it "rhetorical analysis"; he applies it to several more group experiences, including a long-term group analytic psychotherapy, in which he explores the group's use of metaphors and the adoption of stimulating and imaginative way of interacting with each other's stories. In another group scenario, he concludes with a commentary on the concept of rhetoric as it occurs in society, social sciences, and therapy scenarios. His analysis is exhaustive and he repeatedly draws on many literary and scholarly sources in taking us beyond the obvious to think about the fertile ways we express ourselves and the multiple and varied ways we find our own metaphors and idioms for what we think and feel, especially in the ways we do it for the benefit of each other.

Martin draws on positioning and dialogical self-theory to delve into the dynamics of human relationships. Once again he gets beyond the obvious and explores the complexities of where we "position" ourselves or are positioned, and all that is encompassed in what we call "self", which becomes the basis of the narrative we adopt in our social intercourse, and, more pointedly, in clinical dialogue, and, most critically, in therapeutic groups where it is essential that we use language and engagement for the ends of inducing hope and healing. Terms such as "cultural baggage ... cargo ... unique individuality ... communality" jump out at me to appreciate what Martin is getting at. We bring so much to our social interactions in terms of our positons, beliefs, ideas, and identifications, and if we get it right we sort it out for civilised discourse and to serve mutual interests. The alternative runs the risk of being blinded by our past griefs and prejudices to be uncivil, ill-tempered, and harmful in our interactions with each other. It has been my experience that when people come together in groups for help, especially therapeutic groups, individuals are remarkably sensible and sensitive. With enlightened leadership, Weegmann demonstrates all the essential elements for how this works. He provides marvelous examples of this in daily life, and more particularly, in therapeutic groups.

In an intriguing venture into matters of monsters, Martin reminds us of their importance in our environs and in ourselves. As he argues, "Monsters mirror something of how humans envisage and construct preferred identities at a human and group level, although cannot be reduced as mere projections of ourselves, as they too (however imaginary they are) influence who we are." He lists the alternatives as to what we do with them—slay, be warned, imprison, segregate, photograph, or treat. Monsters embody the challenges of our best and worst images of self and other. I leave it to the reader to position or place himself or herself in the imageries of awe, horror, curiosity, and rejection as to where Weegmann says monsters take us.

Once again Martin skilfully traces these themes through the centuries wherein each successive generation and culture found ways and terms to demonise and terrorise "external others", as part of a means to assure one's own sense of legitimacy and power. For example, this was the case for Christendom whether it be Islamic or Jewish others. Weegmann draws out more specifically how and why this was the case with the Jews. Martin does this with stimulating information and insights on the persistent human need to distrust and hate (other) and "us-them" polarisations. Subsequently he similarly explores the fascination, disdain, and diminishment with and about "other" as the New

World opened to the West. The fear aspects of these themes then play out in the creation or birth of Frankenstein and the imagery of Gothic and science fiction. Weegmann suggests the imagery of monsters, thus generated, "appear[s] in literature and political writings to signal both a terrible threat to established rules and a call to arms that demands the confirmation and protection of authorised values" (Botting, 1991, p. 47). In this context he informs us where curiosity with and derision of deformity and "freaks" derive from. Indeed, what a sad and troubling saga about our human nature in the need to set ourselves apart from "other".

Martin, in seeking permission to narrate, moves on to the story of Alcoholics Anonymous. He knows well whereof he speaks and is astutely aware of the benefits for those who come and remain in the programme; furthermore, because of his immersion with AA, he has been honoured by the Home Office as one of their non-recovering trustees. He reminds us that Alcoholics Anonymous is grounded in story-telling traditions. It is well-suited for individuals who are lost for words about their feeling and thoughts, who are lonely and cut-off (a patient of mine described himself as a "born again isolationist"), who have great shame and shattered self-esteem, and who are unaccustomed or unable to ask for help. As cause and effect, they have opted for and have settled on chemical solutions and attachment to alcohol and other substances in place of human ones. Weegmann appreciates well how "immersion" in the programme stimulates a reversal of this process, and opens a new narrative of change and recovery. The shared experiences kindle a basis to solve common problems and help others. Notwithstanding the controversies, successful ideas can stir, and AA has not escaped them. Martin and I are vividly aware, based on our observation and experience, how the programme not only can remove the obsession to drink but, more remarkably, produces personal growth and transformation for those who can adhere to it. Although AA in not psychotherapy, it truly is therapeutic. Martin treats the reader to an analysis and explanation as to how this is so after providing a brief description of the development and evolution of AA.

Martin next takes on issues of social and political revolution. He offers: "revolutions kick-start new narratives", a delightful way to get into these domains. Martin and I share Marxist links. My father embraced revolutionary ideas because he was so convinced the world was unjust and needed drastic changes about wealth, oppression, and inequality. Martin found it at university as an alternative to the conservative world of his parents. Fortunately, we both found an alternative narrative and vehicle to produce change and relief of suffering through clinical work, albeit in more modest ways than those espoused by radical revolutionaries. He gets into the "rhetoric" of revolution at the outset because of the fear and exhilaration it provokes. Weegmann submits that revolutionaries are "avengers of injustice". Oh, how at times I wish I could adopt and madly express my indignation in that way about what is wrong in the world. Don't we all periodically want to rebel or revolt for so many reasons? But Martin Weegmann provides avenues and ways of thinking, not always simple, which, apart from revolutionary solutions, can help us find measures of justice and avenues of solace from the oppression that the world imposes or heaps upon us. He traces how these matters have played out over centuries of doctrinal and tyrannical rule by so many monarchs and political figures. Radical solutions take many forms, and unleash a variety of forces, including the tyranny and reactions in these processes of the "ugly and unruly crowds".

In his closing chapters on critiques of psychoanalysis and paradigms for group psychotherapy, Martin Weegmann courageously takes on shibboleths and doctrine of another kind. He starts with his teenage discovery, fascination, and threat that he experienced as he first read Freud and then Marx, both of which were to be hidden from his parents as forbidden material (he calls it "dangerous knowledge"). He explains how he was interested in excavations, at first archaeological ones and then Freud's psychic variety. He describes his explorations of Freud in terms of the "political", wherein simplistic reductions of his theories are avoided, and of feminism, as a movement that provided a radical reappraisal of Freud's ideas by questioning the traditional oedipal scheme and the suggestion that "anatomy is destiny". Drawing on other feminist sources, he describes how he began to question the notion of "stable identity" and affirms the importance of resistance causing a new perception, for example, in Freud's famous case, of "indifferent" Dora as a fighter. Martin gets to his "textual Freud" whereby in the 1980s he is motivated to read Freud in great detail and rigorously, that is, "obsessively and entranced", as he puts it. And finally he accedes to a "literary Freud", namely the enjoyability and excellence of Freud's prose. Drawing on various sources, Martin believes this excellence stimulated a "new discourse", which he further explores. It also motivated him to first embrace his role as "psychoanalytic" and subsequently to tone it down a notch to "psychodynamic".

Weegmann candidly admits to idealisation and arrogance about himself and his psychoanalytic supervisors, which he fortunately relinquishes. He says he learned to moderate his stern psychoanalytic persuasions. This is something like the joke I make that I am a "recovering psychoanalyst", when I became impatient with doctrinaire and obscure interpretations. He ends his discourse on Freud's contribution, including an appraisal of Freud's book on group psychology as classic, and describes the influences of Foulkes and Foucault on his thinking and work as a group analyst. He concludes here with a commentary on heroes and heroines and "fascination", and links these refrains to the cult of celebrity and elevation of psychoanalytic figures. I am reminded of Arnold Goldberg's book *The Prisonhouse of Psychoanalysis*, the title of which is telling enough, but, more to the point, our penchant, as Goldberg put it, is for an addiction to theory (and by implication, theorists) and confusing the message with the messenger. Whatever our academic or professional persuasions, don't we all need periodic right-sizing?

I hope this is a good guide for the reader to pursue this exceptional piece of narrative and exploration of the varied and far-ranging issues he tackles. I conclude by saying that in his final chapter he brings his same vigour and scrutiny to critiquing the evolution of group analysis, and his assertion that it risks stagnation and needs, as he puts it, "new sources and disciplines, so as to better engage with the world as it is now". He incisively offers creative suggestions and new means to achieve this end.

Professor Edward J. Khantzian, MD
Harvard Medical School
Boston, Massachusetts

INTRODUCTION

"All life is an experiment. The more experiments you make the better."

—*Ralph Waldo Emerson*, 11 November 1842 (2007)

"And, strange to tell, among the Earthen Lot
Some could articulate, while others not:
And suddenly one more impatient cried—
"Who is the Potter, pray, and who the Pot?"

—*Rubáiyát* of Omar Khayyám, *LX*, originally eleventh
century (1992)

I have always liked words and the astonishing things we can do with them. It may stem from sensitivity, as I found that words could wound me, but that they could also afford a measure of protection, even if whispered, in secret, to myself. Words are not apart from, but are integral to action, to our impact and presence, to showing and seeing. Words are felt. We do not invent language as individuals, yet in learning it we take it in to the innermost folds of personal life; baptised in its waters, we clutch it as it clutches us. We name with it, and are named. As speaking subjects were are dispersed, "speaking from" and "spoken by" the discourses that precede, surround, and follow us. Words might be part of our equipment in the world, but we are equally *its* subjects. Whichever way round, however, speech surely is, as rhetorician Gorgias put it, a most "powerful lord".

Permission to Narrate is deeply concerned with questions of language, position, and articulation. I take the evocative phrase of the title from an essay of Edward Said (1984), writing of systematic efforts to reduce Palestinian existence, a people moreover invited to participate in the dismantling of their own history; history is written by victors, not the vanquished, it is often said. The wider truth within Said's term is deep in so far as it invites us to consider questions about who speaks and how, under what conditions and with what implications. The vanquished answer back, creating counter-narratives and alternate positions, however fragile and adverse their conditions of emergence. Hegemony involves semiotic domination, as people, groups, and individuals are caught in, and out, by the struggles of history. A good instance of counter-narrative and research in the socio-academic world is that of the "history from below" movement, in which popular and working-class history was published. And some subjects suffer double invisibility, are subjects behind subjects, as in the case of women's subordination, as explored by Shelia Rowbotham (1973). To "claim" such subjects— bodies, if one wills—from occlusion and marginality involves narrative struggle as well as many other efforts.

As with such examples of alternative history, I have increasingly come to regard psychotherapy as a form of permission to narrate, as the space within which those dominated by their problems can better locate how things came to be that way, to see themselves anew, and in so doing they might come to tell and experience their lives differently. The weight of given history is lifted. Alternative versions. Redress. It is not only a matter of learning how to speak, but, frequently, of "unlearning not to speak" (Gilbert & Gubar, 1979, p. 84).

Years ago I used to think that some people were "articulate" and others not. You either had it or did not. An absolute. I no longer hold with this, as I see the human mind as a literary mind, so that we all, without exception, use distinct grammars of expression, inventive metaphors, expressive rhetoric, engaging prose. We use particular idioms to signify ordinary and extra-ordinary experience, suffering, pleasure, achievement, experiences of each and every kind. This does not arise by magic, but is sculpted by the materials that are at hand and by our life experiences; Khayyám was right—tangled creatures that we are, we are both "potter and pot".

Therapy is one of the places to which people turn when they are dissatisfied with the direction of their lives. It is one context amongst others, and in terms of an act of talking about oneself it is a context, seldom an absolute start, even if we might be new to it. I take careful note of how people express themselves, from the start, in its particular forms. In general I find that clients are more than adept at suiting "action to word, the word to the action", as Shakespeare put it, notwithstanding the difficulties and concerns that bring them to help in the first place. An "ever-increasing articulation" was S. H. Foulkes' useful phrase, but it does not mean that at the outset clients lack this essential quality. Therapy provides an opportunity for redress, a recourse for knowing ourselves in a new way. And as a new context, we can take what the context gives us into ourselves, into the innermost regions.

The chapters

The first two chapters are concerned with the contours, role, and content of language as it appears in groups, including the speech acts and the positions of the speaking subject. A modern theory of rhetoric is explored, tied as it is to the performative aspects of human life—the hows of speech and not just its content. How do we "shape" and "give voice" to our experiences? The second chapter examines positioning theory, with its rich invitation to dwell upon the notion of self-as-dialogue, in conditions of power, with its competing characters, voices, authors, and the related metaphor of self as society.

Monsters have interested me for a long while and are the subject of the third chapter. Monsters are effectively "intimate strangers" who follow us and spring up in all manner of regions; they also evolve, disappear, and mutate within culture. It is argued that, in their manifold ways, monsters connect deeply with issues of cultural position, definition, and to how we narrate ourselves as human subjects and locate our place within the world and natural order.

Chapter Four explores the role of narratives of recovery from alcoholism, using Alcoholics Anonymous as an example. AA began in mid-America in the 1930s, a time when stigma and marginalisation of alcoholics was widespread, and, arguably, post-prohibition America was ripe for a "new paradigm" of care. It was fitting, therefore, that a mutually organised fellowship of men and women arose, whose basic principle was one alcoholic helping another. AA meetings are structured in distinct ways, within which anyone can have their say, in speech acts known as "sharing". AA constitutes a narrative community through which lifestyles of recovery are forged.

Chapter Five analyses the subject of revolution—its subjects, bodies, and crowds. Kick-started by reading Harold Behr's (2015) study of the French revolution, mine is a cultural essay that situates the topic of revolution in a wider context, including the English revolution. Revolutions change the ways people see and act in the world and are a decisive break from "old order" narratives. They institute a radical break, a new story.

Chapter Six is semi-autobiographical and explores a range of refractions through which I have related to Freud and psychoanalysis over time. I also reflect on the nature of fascination, idealisation, and its consequences. My conclusion, unexceptional perhaps, is that much as I value psychoanalytic traditions—although from a heterodox persuasion—I do not afford it the same privilege as I once did and nor do I think psychoanalysis has a monopoly on that which is deep or foundational within our natures.

The final chapter pushes forward a hypothesis that I have been working on for some time, and which I began in my previous book, *The World Within the Group* (2014a). In that book I argue that the founding paradigm and dependencies of group analysis are exhausted, or were always too limited, to enable bold and creative new work in the discipline. In response to our struggling and declining influence, we might be tempted to take a road of retreat and isolation, splendid or otherwise, but that will only compound the problem. Alternatively, we can embrace the need for paradigm change, and draw sustenance from new sources and disciplines, so as to better engage with the world as it is now.

On a personal note

At Sussex University I was blessed by an interesting teaching structure that included "contextuals" alongside a degree subject, which in my case was developmental psychology. One of my first contextuals was "critical reading", which introduced me to novels by Orwell, Huxley, and—one that stood out—Edmund Gosse's *Father and Son*.

Father and Son is about generational differences and incommensurable world-views—Gosse's father is a naturalist and Plymouth Brethren, committed to a literalist view of the Bible, whist the young Gosse comes to reject religion, embraces the ideas of Darwin, and embarks on a career as a writer. This resonated with my struggle to displace the world of my parents, although Marxism, rather than evolution, played the major part in that differentiation. Rather than attached to a traditional school of psychology, at Sussex we were located in a hybrid known as cultural and community studies. Contextuals took me into many realms, as did my political passions, on the Left, and I found myself preferring such excursions to the dryness (as I then saw it!) of developmental psychology. Of course, an interest in all things revolutionary and alternative was part of that Sussex scene. I still believe that to understand anything one should look around its edges, and not always straight on, and, often as not, to unlikely, shadow, adjacent regions of knowledge.

After a long time in the resistance, I finally made friends with psychology and became a clinical psychologist. Also a psychotherapist (group analyst), I value a professional dual-citizenship whereby I can develop long-held analytic interests alongside the requirements of a disciplined, rigorous profession, not that these two characteristics are that simply characterised, nor are they mutually excluding. Literature too, in the form of novels, plays, and poetry, has influenced my practice deeply. I have found an inter-feed between them so that one day I can trust a soar of associative imagination and another day consult research papers, one day find inspiration in poetic and literary sources and another be close to the ground, to immediate exigencies of peoples" lives, these perspectives well and truly tangled. Not that I do this on whim, but, hopefully, in being responsive to that which is most helpful for clients. I might have damned the very mention of the word "empirical" at university, but now welcome it, "pragmatism" even more so, but I do not think psychology should be afraid of the literary realm. The fact that I have moved more towards a narrative approach in my practice is testimony to the fact that I believe it can satisfy different requirements and is non-exclusive in this respect.

Most of my professional life thus far has been devoted to working with individuals suffering from substance misuse and those with personality disorders, including the families they live with. Seen as "difficult clients", and tagged "complex", I prefer to see them as "especially troubled" by complicating life experiences and consequences. For one reason or another (I've never got to the bottom of it, if that is even possible) I have been drawn to work with those who live *in extremis* and around social margins; I have learned more about human nature and nurture, frailty and strength from these populations than from any other. They have been my best teachers.

Recovery from such disorders is unpredictable, surprising, and wondrous, and takes many different forms. I am grateful for an opportunity to train in the "recovery approach" with one of its inspirations, the psychologist Dr. Rachel Perkins, in south west London. I am also grateful to Alcoholics Anonymous, an organisation to whom I am close as a professional friend (and a "non-alcoholic trustee" with their general services board), for giving me insights into the world of change—the opening of new chapters, new starts, new narratives.

It will be apparent from these chapters that I do not stay within the tramlines of normal disciplinary boundaries and that I maintain critical distance from any given tradition, be it theoretical, therapeutic, and so forth. I have always felt a fear of being taken over by any singular authority, again for reasons that are hard to fathom, but it has, I trust, served me fairly well. In fact, I call myself an "undisciplinable", to use William James' magnificent expression.

To realise one's own authority takes a long time, and despite personal and professional achievements there have been many areas of life in which I have felt inadequate and unable to quite "get behind" my voice. That reticence is no longer an issue. Partly through the discipline of writing, I have granted myself "permission to narrate".

This introduction begins with quotations, the first that of essayist Ralph Waldo Emerson. His valuation of experiments and metaphor of paths appeals to my sense of pragmatism and individuality. I have always made things—with words, through art, and other outlets. All help me to break beyond the exaggerated conventionality with which I was raised, with its anxious emphasis on not making a fuss and upon conformity. And so too the chapters are experiments of sorts— promptings, applications, and critical reflections. Most of all I hope they leave interesting trails ...

All clinical material is of a composite nature.

CHAPTER ONE

The rhetorical ground of group analysis

T his chapter gives an outline of how the term "rhetoric" is regarded in classical and in modern times. Originally seen as eloquence and the art of persuasion, including misleading speech, rhetoric nowadays has a wider application to all spheres of communication—in how we are called upon, answer and address others, including the uses of an infinite variety of acts of speech. A contemporary theory of rhetoric has much to offer in terms of providing a deeper understanding of the communications that take place in the therapy group.

In describing the development of articulate language in group therapy, Foulkes (1966, p. 156) emphasises *"work* in communication" (italics in the original). The metaphor of work is a familiar one in psychoanalytic discourse, as in "dream-work", "work of mourning", "working-through", and so on. I say metaphor deliberately, as the work in question postulates a raw material (e.g., the dream, symptoms, experience of loss, etc.) that like other materials is resistive to, but also changed by being subject to, analysis.[1] In previous work (Weegmann, 2014a), reviewing various gaps at the heart of group analysis, I addressed "communication", which while central to Foulkes is undeveloped as a theory; I argued that narrative approaches are one way to develop that theory. The narrative shape we give to our experiences and lives is

1

closely tied to *how* we address and speak. So much can be learned from closer inspection of the uses in group discourse of emphasis, tense, metaphor, tropes, speech acts, communion, accommodation, and so forth. A modern theory of rhetoric can thus lift a rather flattened notion of communication into a richer, more variegated conception of group dialogue. Our understanding of the nature of "work in communication" is similarly deepened.

Foulkes (1974, p. 279), without ever using words such as rhetoric or aesthetic, acknowledged the "creative function" of the therapist: "I have sometimes compared this function to that of the poet, especially in conducting a group." Such a function is hardly confined to the therapist, and modern views of rhetoric take notions of performance, including aesthetic aspects of human life, into the centre of its account. Although traditionally associated with the spoken word and the art of discourse, modern rhetoric theory is more extensive and interdisciplinary in scope.

Rhetoric's renewal

The concept of rhetoric has undergone several sea changes in the history of philosophy. Just as Aristotle's *Poetics* (1997) is a foundational text in terms of the concept of narrative, so his *Rhetoric* (2004) was an important defence of the ancient "art of persuasion", and a response to its critics, notably Plato. Plato saw the rhetorical arts as little more than misleading speech, hence his use of the accusatory term "sophistry", directed against the so-called Sophist philosophers. Adopting a narrowed concept of rhetoric as speech-making, Plato dismisses the basis of its appeal as one stemming from mere opinion, divorced from true knowledge. As we shall see, this attack on rhetoric as opinion, knack, and flattery found echoes in other philosophies down the centuries, but before we elaborate, let us consider the alternative position of Aristotle, whose more positive views on the subject also had a long afterlife.

Aristotle confined his intervention to the then prevalent notion of rhetoric as staged speech and means of persuasion, in several contexts, such as law or politics. Rhetoric was the art of discourse and was an increasing necessity in Greek social life, as, for example, persuasive demonstration was required in the settling of legal disputes in the courts over land. He who delivers the speech is a participant in a structure of discourse and persuasion, dependent on an audience (e.g., a jury). In a detailed enumeration of the features of rhetoric, Aristotle outlines its subtle features, including what it says about the character of the speaker, the audience addressed, and the modes of demonstration and proof that are used. Speech needs to be credible and appropriate in its use of the emotions, and so on. Hence, "speaker, subject, and the person addressed" are central to Aristotle's (2004) definition; he argues that rhetoric should not be counterposed to knowledge or truth. His "technical" discussions of styles, figures, and composition of prose and speech are fascinating, as is his exploration of its "five canons": invention, arrangement, style, memory, and delivery.

In the medieval and Renaissance periods, rhetoric was revived. Connected to social or civic life, the "noble art" was intimately linked to the cultivation of eloquent speech in the education of privileged, usually, males. In the curriculum of the medieval university, one sphere of learning (so-called *trivium*) comprised the disciplines of grammar, logic, and rhetoric, with debates about which should have greater priority. In the tradition of Renaissance humanism, Italian philosopher Vico, mounted a defence of rhetoric and its cardinal importance in the education of youth. Manuals and guidance on the art of "showing" and conducting oneself in conversation abounded in Italy, France, and Britain, from the sixteenth century to the eighteenth century (Burke, 1993).

Meanwhile, views hostile to rhetoric were held by others, as in the philosophy of Locke (1689/2009) who argued that rhetoric is the "artificial and figurative application of words" and one that shades into the dark art of wit and deceit. Such views had social significance,[2] so that, for example, the English Quakers of the seventeenth century advocated the use of "plain speech" (and "plain style") in accordance with a view of the primacy of inner experience and rejection of the "outwardly" (e.g., ritual, embellishment, image, etc.). Theirs is a form of "direct Christianity", of "that of God in everyone", and was based on a radical critique of social hierarchy, sermon, priests, and church structure (Collins, 2001). Speech got in the way of direct experience, as detour or as "idle talk", hence the Quaker cultivation of silence and waiting. One early Quaker leader, James Naylor, saw human languages as ultimately obfuscations from the "eternal word" of God, a view consonant with the Biblical idea that, in the beginning, "the whole world was of one language, of one speech" (Genesis 11: 1–9; Guiton, 2012). Ironically, however, Quaker plain was no more than the invention of a new form of rhetoric, with its own distinctive style and conventions (Collins, 2001).

Modern developments in rhetoric

- In modern use, rhetoric is no longer confined to staged speech or oratory, and finds a wide base within theories of language and communication. In the nineteenth century, Nietzsche presaged this expansion by displacing rhetoric as conscious employment of artistic speech and relocating it at the heart of *all* language. "What is usually called language", in the Nietzschean position, "is actually all figuration" (Nietzsche, 1872–73, p. 25). In this view, language is not so much literal as always and creatively pointing to itself, to its other terms and devices.

- Rhetoric theory was transformed by its incorporation within philosophies of language in the twentieth century. Wittgenstein's later philosophy of language was a decisive move away from his earlier picture theory of language as based on precision and logical proposition. Instead he developed the radical notion of "language games", in which the meaning of statements is not fixed but is intimately dependent on context, use, and the rules that specify that usage. There are no limits, in principle, to meaning, and meaning is always connected to the "forms of life" (*Lebensform*) within which it is embedded. The evocative term "game" capitalises on this sense of play, rule, and convention in language (Wyse, 1996).

- An influential development is that of "speech act" theory. According to its originator, Austin (1962), words are acts that "show" and "do" as much as they "say", and are inseparable from the contingences of context. Words and sentences have an intrinsic performative function, for example, as question, command, request, apology, criticism, complaint, and many others. Words have an "illocutionary force", in that in their saying they enact something and thus have outcomes on the social relations in which they take place (Norris, 1983).

- The expansion of rhetorical studies—the creation of the "new rhetoric"—is also indebted to the American literary theorist Kenneth Burke. Albeit it difficult work to read, and idiosyncratic, one of his innovations is the centrality he accords to identification, and not just the role of "persuasion" in the old rhetoric. Identification through language is critical to the formation and maintenance of social life, by acts of naming, definition, and the provision of shareable "equipment" for negotiating, consoling, and so forth (e.g., a parable would be one example; Burke, 1998). Most rhetorical resources fall, he suggests, "in an intermediary area of expression, not wholly deliberate yet not unconscious" (Burke, 1969, p. xiii). In other words, human beings draw on them without deliberate planning, in the conversations or situations in which they find themselves.

- Social scientists have contributed considerably to a modern approach to rhetoric, not only philosophers, as we shall see in the work of Goffman.
- Cognitive neuroscientists Lakoff and Johnson (1980) researched the suffusion of metaphor in everyday life, those "metaphors we live by". In an incisive comment, they remark: "Metaphor is for most people a device of the poetic imagination and the rhetorical flourish—a matter of extraordinary rather the ordinary language" (p. 3); the opposite is the case. Their examples demonstrate how our basic conceptual system is metaphorical in nature, structuring our very perception and thinking. Turner's (1996) work, in a similar vein, proposes a model of the "literary mind" and the complex relationships and mapping between the cognitive and the linguistic domain. His book traces the role of mental images as building blocks for narrative competencies. Meaning is not fixed once and for all, deposited as it were in a concept-container. Instead, it is "alive and active, dynamic and distributed. ... complex operations of projection, binding, linking, blending, and integration over multiple spaces" (p. 57). "Blended spaces" is how he describes this creative, ever-changing aspect.
- "Discursive psychology" is a productive paradigm of research and theory, which makes a considerable contribution to how we might think of human selves. Take as but one instance, that of conceiving "voice" in human interaction and discourse. When we refer to "finding voice", or "giving voice to . ....", or "speaking out", we are referring to what is in actuality a complex performance within intimate contexts of language use. It may involve power relations, in which a person (or group) struggles with a lack of authority, even "rights" to speech, which, to be overcome, involves articulation of new space within language. The voice has not only stable properties, such as tone, but dynamic ones involving presence and sense of agency—for example, we may vary in how much we speak up in one situation as compared to another, betraying confidence in one domain and uncertainty in another. A useful angle for understanding these dimensions, with implications for intergroup and interpersonal relations, is the work of Giles (Giles, Coupland & Coupland, 1991) and his associates

who emphasise processes of accommodation, convergence, and divergence within language. More recently, in "On linguistic vulnerability", Butler (1997) explores the sense of dramatic agency we ascribe to language (building upon, amongst other sources, speech act theory), and, in her particular focus, its power to injure and hurt (e.g., hate crime). In such cases, linguistic and physical vocabularies may combine, as in the idea of being "subject to verbal assault" or in saying "it was like a slap in the face".

• The work of Loughborough University "Discourse and rhetoric group" over the last twenty-five years has been described as a "quiet revolution" in social psychology. Their research has helped reconceive psychology in broadly socio-discursive terms, exploring how humans, "produce, debate, resist and implicate versions of minds, worlds and social relationships" (Augoustinos & Tileaga, 2012, p. 206).

The discursive space of group therapy

Social life is full of transitions and switches in which the nature of conversation changes. This may reflect a change in levels of formality and ethos of particular practices, as people switch from one situation to another and as illustrated by the case of group therapy.

Example

The setting was an in-patient, detoxification ward with clients coming off alcohol and/or drugs, staying for approximately two to three weeks. I ran a weekly group, entitled "Where Next?", one of a number of groups in the ward programme.

On the day in question, the nursing staff began "rounding up" (collecting patients from the day area, bedrooms, etc.). There was a climate of protest, one person complaining that he had "done it before", another asking "Well what's this one about?" and a third that he was tired and did not like "pointless talking". Others readied themselves and, protest aside, patients slowly gathered in the group room. A newcomer (clients would typically attend up to three times during the course of their stay) asked if this was "another of those OT [occupational therapy] things?". His quick-witted peer retorted, "No, he's not as good looking as her!" Once introductions were completed, together with a description of the purpose of the group, the climate changed, with focus on discussion about the future. "I'm here to put my house in order," one said. "We might be in it together, but I have to make it alone," added another.

Discussion

Dynamics such as these at the start of this group will be familiar to those who work in detoxification, and indeed in other in-patient settings. Initial reluctance is common, although, notwithstanding, is frequently resolved and recedes once the group is underway. "Crossing the threshold" and settling people in a formal group situation is therefore the first task. In terms relevant to communication, it can be said that the group carves formal discursive space, which is interruptive of the informal spaces from which the patients have been called, including awoken from. The informal voices that sound down corridors are of course also meaningful expressions of socialisation and solidarity between patients—for example, ward gossip, small talk, behind the back criticism, and so forth. Lefebvre (1991) refers to the fact that, "every language is located in space. Every discourse says something about space (place or sets of places); and every discourse is emitted from a space" (p. 132). What can be said, and how, rhetorical expression, or its inhibition, indeed "language switching" (e.g., informal to formal), is tied to specific locales, such as, in this case, the ward.

The language of pre-group protest (or inquiry) is directed at the nurses. I will not dwell on the dynamic aspects of this, which includes power relations—for example, nurses remind and cajole/enforce, patients complain/resist (for more on the psychodynamic aspects of ward life, see Weegmann, 2011). "Done it before" conjures up a routine, nameless experience (an "it"), indistinguishable from other "its" (other groups) in the week; the implication is that an experience "done" once is of no continuing interest. His subject-position implies a stance of removal, "this need not apply to me". "What's this one about?" might suggest reluctance, and/or a form of inquiry, directed at the nurses, who inform him of the group name. Seen as a form of inquiry, he may be trying to sort out how this particular group fits in to the programme and the nature of its possible demand upon him. It should be remembered that patients are often disoriented and physically uncomfortable, living within a brief, temporary community with (mostly) strangers; staff members are also new faces, unless that person had been admitted before (not uncommon). "What's this one about?" may slide into a question of names; group names, including the person with whom the group is associated, are signifiers. They gather its purpose together. Finally, "pointless talking" communicates a different kind of resistance and a polarity: pointless/purposeful. This invites a persuasive counter-response from nurses, who would typically react by underlining its relevance. In this context, the art of persuasion has a practical, immediate dimension. The ward is a good example of what could be called the operation of a "sociology of knowledge", in so far as a therapeutic culture is reproduced all the time, on an everyday basis and part of this includes legitimation—for example, "the programme" requires a rationale, an accessible justification of why this needs to be done.

Once inside the room, just before introductions, a newcomer asks if it is "another of those OT things?" Once again, there is an association to and a naming of an entity, similar or different to the group at hand. His subject position is that of the newcomer, figuring something out in reference to something else of which he has had an experience. Definitions gain credence and validity within the community in which they are articulated, and are rendered useful or otherwise. Using Wittgenstein, once might say that they involve "family resemblances", a process of creating typology and likeness, for example, is a psychology group like the OT group? Such group referents are part of an informal vocabulary and language game, just as professionals have these as part of their rhetoric of purpose (e.g., the official group name and introductory statements about the aims of the group and so forth) designed to bring clients swiftly on board. Our commonplaces (the language we use, and referents, etc.) will not be the same as those used by patients.

His peer cracks a joke, whereby OT groups are associated with an attractive female therapist, and my status is reduced by the comparison, with an added twist of gender. The person who makes the joke gains rhetorical presence as an "experienced" patient on the ward (relative to a newcomer), a wit maybe, with the joke illustrating the exercise of informal authority. I have never ceased to be amazed by the generative powers of dialogue, in which someone's response moves instantly to occupy the briefest of gaps in conversation. In a humorous aside such as this, serious discourse is temporarily suspended and impoliteness is expressed in an acceptable manner. Humour and "off-record speech acts" are essential features of conversation, and take the edge off situations or emotions (Mulkay, 1988; Pinker, 2007).[3] In this case, his repartee marks a distinction (a "no") and shoots through any pretentions I might have; I happen to take the downsizing of my authority on the chin, although embarrassment—on my part, for such a comparison, or the newcomer, for his naivety—were both possible. Instead, in this case, we both laughed and relaxed, and so in fact it, and our reactions, proved a useful bridge and switch point into the formal discursive space of the group.

With the group underway, there was a more concentrated atmosphere reflecting the manner in which I comport myself and "explain" the task at hand. I say "explain", but, given my style, it is as much about the spirit in which the group is facilitated as any explicit articulation of its purpose, but also this is a relational reality in which how patients begin to express themselves also creates the norm in which the discussion ensues. The therapist sets the tone. "I'm here to put my house in order" is an interesting metaphor, connoting responsibility (the opposite in positioning terms to telling someone *else* to put their house in order) and implies personal or psychological work—to attend to one's difficulties, to make progress, bring order out of chaos, and so on. Others identify with this. "We might be in it together, but I have to make it alone" says another, in an interesting articulation of this struggle and play on the pronouns "We"/"I". It connotes a common problem ("We all have the same kind of problem") and an "I" of personal responsibility ("I have to create my own path of recovery"). It is a double-positioning, that of a person acknowledging the common suffering of a shared disorder (in this case addiction) and that of a person who has to choose their own course of action. His remark reminded me of a therapeutic community saying, "I alone can do it, but I can't do it alone", which I cited. The client, in talking about himself, was offering the gift of what might be called a "saying"; a saying is an adage, or principle, which other people will know to be true when they hear it. Such sayings and other poetic styles promote identification and communion.

Sayings can bond groups, as they "go through" people whilst at the same time addressing them, and have a way of combining a universal with a particular (hence the notion of "timeless wisdom"). By my sharing of a recovery expression, I amplified the importance of the client's personal statement whilst drawing upon a wider discursive resource, that of the cultural capital of recovery traditions and wisdom. Groups balance communication, where different viewpoints are explored and change initiated, and communion, which involves sharing and maintenance of connections. In the case of sayings, resonance is created, as they "hit home", are "home truths", indeed offer a "home" for meaning.

In a very real sense those with substance problems have to learn (re-learn) the art of "sober dialogue", which I (Weegmann & English, 2010, p. 8) have defined as "improved contact and toleration of different parts of the self and others". The speaking skills required for (early) recovery are basic communicative competencies, including listening, respectful expression, and self-reflection. What remains remarkable, all the same, about one-off groups such as the one described is just how quickly a group of strangers in difficult circumstances can and do create meaningful, purposeful dialogue.

I do not take the view that the contrasting rhetoric of corridors and informal space versus that of the therapy group is explained by a process of "splitting". This notion is easily over-applied and a more plausible explanation may pertain to what Goffman (1981) calls "regions" and "region behaviour", within various "interaction orders". According to Goffman, not only behaviour but speech differs according to the "stage" on which it occurs. Familiarity, jokes, "in-group" lingo, and so on are reserved for the "back stage" of informal areas, with greater formality of speech occurring in the "front stage" of the therapy room. Staff also have "off stage" areas where they talk differently, relax, joke, and so forth, such as the nursing office. Language and its contexts of use, the accommodations, identifications and distinctions it provides for, are continually reproduced as part of such interaction orders.

Voice and rhetorical power

A capacity so basic to humans that it is easy to overlook is the fact of being able to attest to experiences, "being able to say" (Ricoeur, 1992). This capacity is more than possessing the gift of language, but involves the ability to produce and to be immersed within complex, spontaneous, and on-going discourses—to have discursive presence and agency. However, our capacity for saying and for narrative identity is never complete, as there is always something more to say, it can be told differently, and, importantly, told by others who have their say on our say, as companions in meaning, which, in a group, takes place in front of us. Life is a forever articulated journey.

In phonetics, articulation refers to how the speech organs (lips, tongue, etc.) "make contact", whereas it is used more generally to refer to a joined state or formation (as in, "articulation of a new thought").

In psychotherapy the term has positive connotations, is a feature of "psychological mindedness" ("He is an articulate client", as distinct from the negatively toned, "There is something inarticulate about her"). In group analysis, Foulkes (1948, p. 169) placed a premium on the idea of the group "working towards ... ever more articulate form[s] ...", and elsewhere (Foulkes & Anthony, 1957, p. 263) he says, "... the group can be compared to a child learning to speak". In spite of the "child learning to talk" analogy, clients of group analysis *already* know how to talk and so the term "articulate" is clearly relative to context or occasion. It is useful to add the notion of voice to that of articulation.

The concept of voice allows a way forward, in particular the notion of voicing to bring in the verb from. Voice suggests something more than tone/pitch (voice quality) or stance (the attitude of the author towards the audience, topic, etc.), but involves a dynamic sense of agency and presence (Jacobs, 1996). Not that there is any simple, expressive relationship of voice to self either. Instead, when we "give voice to", "find voice", "speak out", and so on, in a real sense we are making ourselves present, through dialogue, in the very act of expression. And we are "multi-voiced", not singular beings, with collective voices helping to constitute individual ones, which brings in the question of power (Hermans, 2001). Feminism and a range of other critical movements have amply demonstrated the power of discursive positioning, struggles around definition, and of vastly differing ranges of "who is allowed to speak and when".

The plot thickens: rhetorical dimensions of group analysis

The following scenarios, from long-term, group-analytic psychotherapy, consider the ways in which rhetorical analysis might help us to understand the subtleties of what is going on in what is being said.

Scenario A

A group returns after the holiday. Feelings about returning are explored. Norman is tentative and fears having to "face things again", the summer having been somewhat of "a respite". Pat joined in, saying she too felt mixed about returning. Sally spoke at greater length about her holiday on the (English) coast where there had been rumours of a Great White Shark. People were entertained by her story, to which she added, nonchalantly, "I suppose that if you're going to get bitten, you're going to get bitten." Pat winced. I said, "Like stepping back into the waters of the group?", to which people smiled. Pat took up the talk to speak of the "different emotional extremes" she had experienced over summer: "I sometimes feel full of energy, full of life, but then I crash and hit that brick wall again." She relates it to her marriage and to long-term despondency. She expresses disquiet that she is "wittering on and on", but Sally encourages her: "It's good to take time in the group, that's why we're here."

Comment

This extract illustrates the presence of several metaphors and metonymies in everyday speech, such as that of "face" (to look at), "things" (emotions, one's life), "shark" (threat), "get bitten" (fortune and tribulations), "crash" (falter), "brick wall" (obstacle), and so on. They are not decorative features of an otherwise essential speech, or simply reflections of some other area of life (such as "the emotions") but are part of its very make-up. My words, too, involve metaphors and descriptions, so that in referring to the "waters of the group" I articulate a theme of re-entering the group and the various anxieties associated to it, which is a play within language.[4] The impact of meaning is a complex and indeterminate process, as in the example of a non-verbal response (Norman's wince) to a situation that although he (most likely) will never encounter—but this is not the point—he can identify with in some way, for example, as a situation representing grave uncertainty. In discourses, we participate in micro- seconds, led by language and reactions beyond ourselves. Language grounds us through a homing of meaning, whilst leading us beyond what we expect, as it forms, unfolds, and reforms itself. Language allows us to identify with others, to be consubstantial, and allows us to differ, to mark ourselves off, in loops of communication that do not cease (see Burke's 1969 theory of rhetorical identification); communication and communion actively combine.

Scenario B

The same group, on another occasion:
Sally reports "tragic news" about the death of a cousin and apprehension about the funeral. Condolences are offered. She admits to being afraid to tell the group in case she becomes too upset: "I'll take the

whole group up if I do." She detailed the circumstances of the cousin's overdose and her anger about the death. She asks Norman, looking pensive, how he is. He describes a difficult situation at college, during a "boring lecture", but hesitated to supply details. With encouragement he does so, explaining that he experiences "aggressive impulses—my demons". He blushes and reports that he wants to shout abuse at the lecturer—"I was about to explode". Norman said similar feelings happened as a boy, "to swear or say something really bad, that would shock my parents." I talk in general terms about "fear of aggression" and the "search for containment of frightening feelings". Norman, like Sally, reports concerns about "seizing time in the group" and "not wanting to be selfish". Two others join in, one (Mags) talking about "murderous thoughts" about her mother, another (Phil) about dislike of his "over-strict" father, which he has to suppress, and which "makes me feel guilty".

Comment

In supervisory discussion of the group, colleagues felt that the group was communicating well, with strong resonance between members. But what does this mean? The first thing to note is that affects, such as grief and anger, do not usually arise in and of themselves, but emerge within narrative reports—short stories, if one wills, of doing and experience that contextualise and occasion (justify?/prompt?/accompany?) the emotion. There are differing intensities and degrees of arousal, from the acute (Sally and Norman) to the distant (Phil); although thought about in terms of a shifting conversation, such qualities can and do change rapidly—for example, if the conversation refocused on Phil, his degree of affective involvement and expression might also have changed.

Speech act theory considers language as symbolic action, so that action and intent are performed when using and listening to language in context. The language in the context of group analysis is different to that of language used in a shop, philosophy group, or other contexts, is a different kind of discursive space. For one, it is in part premised on the importance of "emotion discourse"—that is, an ideal of communication and "being in touch" with emotions. The speech act involved in the emotion discourse of therapy can be described as "behavities", that is, speech acts that convey an affective stance (e.g., distressed through grief), reflect shared attitudes (e.g., authoritarian fathers are not good for their children), and that invite, in theory, cooperative social responses (e.g., permission, condolence, etc.).

There are differences in the group in question between "talking with" and "talking about" emotion. However, since all feeling is given form the moment it is spoken, it could be argued that once spoken it becomes impossible to close the "gap" between an emotion and a communication, an experiencing self and a narrating self. What constitutes communication includes an inescapable literary equipment, a discursive act with all its cargo of allusion, reference, and ambiguity. The range of human feelings, or desires, is bound up with culture and "in turn is inseparable from the distinctions and categories marked by the language people speak" (Taylor, 1976, p. 165). Communicating emotions reflects our evaluations (e.g., I am justified to feel anger towards my cousin for the circumstances of his death), or goals (e.g., I will try to be more assertive in the future about what I feel), or cognitions (e.g., I have murderous *thoughts* about my mother) in a way that starts to run together, and this includes the body (e.g., the blush). Emotion is expressed by everyday metaphors (e.g., I was about to explode) and employs a large range of rhetorical contrasts and devices (e.g., *tragic* news, not just news, *really* bad, and not just bad), but which also exceeds the individual in question—emotions are part of a conversational trade that others implicitly understand, even if they do not always feel the same way (e.g., we can all relate to grief, even if our culture of response will vary; an overdose, like a suicide, might in the not-so-distant past have been associated to sin, and passed over in silence or strong disapproval, but nowadays might evoke different, no less "authentic", emotion-moral responses, such as "anger at a wasted life", or "saddened by the tragedy", and so on). Emotion connects to voice, to rhetorical presence, as in the shift that occurs when Norman goes from pensive, hesitant group member to (through encouragement) more expressive member who, paradoxically, in speaking already overcomes his fear of "seizing" (interestingly an aggressive metaphor) group time.

Emotional life cannot be separated from the rich and varied vocabularies that accompany it. Language, including languages of emotion, carries deposits of meaning that are characterised by constancy and change (Berger & Luckmann, 1966). Edwards (1999, p. 276), in his research, considers the ways in which emotions are "worked up descriptively rather than simply being the way things were, prior to description". In other words, we use intensifying adjectives, poetic emphasis, and other devices in contexts of "situated talk", a rhetoric of emotions as well as of motives. This applies to the ways of talking and sharing space that occur in group analysis as much as any other speaking-sharing context.

In previous work (Weegmann, 2014a) on narrative dimensions of group life, I have suggested that one of the things we do is create conditions for greater "discursive democracy" amongst group members, a kind of equality in discourse. If psychoanalysis introduced the multiplicity of self (conscious, unconscious, parts of the personality, etc.), group analysis introduces the multiplicity of selves, including varying discursive locations of self, differing subject-positions, and multiple points of subjectivity. We are multi-story beings who, in a group context, are overwritten by others through their responses. Two people at least (Sally and Norman) demonstrate rhetorical uncertainty about taking their share in the democracy (e.g., "taking the whole group up", "seizing group time"), although in the act of so doing, in being responsive one to another, they do bring themselves in. In this respect, groups are remarkable spaces to witness the infinite subtleties, rhythms, turns, intensities, and so on, that language and dialogue provide.

Finally, as for my comments about containment, I wonder if this was a recourse to a favoured psychoanalytic metaphor. Containment suggests a process: contents—container-containment. Psychic life placed somewhere, to/in another space, an inside, and there held, rendered safe. But was this required in the circumstances, given that group communication was already in flow? Was I comforting myself, trying to feel useful? Was I implying, as the psychoanalytic metaphor generally does, a problem, a deficit, something requiring help, such as how people handle or do not handle aggressive impulses or grief reactions? Arguably the containment metaphor is overused, and is too unidirectional, not to mention its traditional associations to maternal functions and infantile needs. Narrative psychology, by contrast, is not problem- and deficit-oriented (White, 2004). So, instead of focusing upon individual selves as cell-like, and contained or otherwise, White's (op. cit., p. 32) notion of a narrative-oriented, folk psychology directs attention to creativity and strengths, to "the potential to throw people's expressions of life into a multiplicity of different lights … difficulties raise options for people to trade in conceptions of personal agency". Perhaps I did not need to talk at all at that juncture.[5]

In practice, it is common for group conductors usually to maintain a "middle voice", allowing a healthy balance of contributions between members and encouraging the play of communication. In this way the group conductor prompts and enables communication to continue and unfold.

Conclusion

This chapter explores the concept of rhetoric, both as seen in philosophy and social science, and as witnessed in the fast traffic of interaction of the therapy group. I argue that such dimensions of speech acts and voice, the compositional aspects of human dialogue, deserve greater attention. We are literary creatures and, in the apt words of Derrida (1988, p. 71), we are also "all mediators, translators".

The clinical examples illustrate something of the way in which subtle exchanges and communications take place. Foulkes did not draw upon any formal theory of, or research on, communication, and so it is important to rethink the language that emerges in groups with such references and wider resources in mind.

Notes

1. The metaphor of analytic work and materials are linked by Freud to the figure of the archaeologist reconstructing long-lost buildings on the basis of buried and revealed fragments (Freud, 1937d).
2. Elias (1978) in his historical review of the development of the emotions, as evidenced in manuals promoting civility, notes that in the changing tactics of struggles between nobles, "each greeting, each conversation has a significance over and above what is actually said or done. They indicate the standing of a person" (p. 271). Humanistic education prepared (mainly) males to lead and to participate with confidence in public life. Many aspects of behaviour were implicated—eloquence, status, politeness, dress, bearing, and so on. Building on Elias, I would suggest that we can learn a great deal from the history of the salon, coffee house, club, and academy in the cultivation of conversation, civility, entertainment, etc., as those regions existed beyond the domain of court and (only) elite society and were critical to a developing, independent "public sector" (Burke, 1993; Habermas, 1989).
3. Indirectness in speech (or indirect speech acts) is critical to a great deal of social interaction, although languages still vary to the degree to which

this is valued. So, for example, irony is used to make a point, amuse, amplify, also to show that the speaker in question is thus "in control of their emotions, and to avoid damaging their relationship with the addressee" (Dews, Kaplan & Winner, 1955, p. 347). Pinker (2007) looks at how "implicatures" in language contribute to social politeness, and its role in innumerable other "off-record" speech acts.

4. Murray Cox expanded our understanding of the role of metaphors in psychotherapy, including the role of "mutative metaphors" (Cox & Theilgaard, 1987). Marratos (2006) offers a summary on the place of myth and metaphor in group analysis.

5. The art of how therapists speak is not commonly addressed in the literature. Reflecting on my style as a trainee, I was at first a minimal, parsimonious speaker, thinking long and hard before I voiced anything and only then trying to deliver precise, encapsulated interpretations. The idea here, modelled on classical analysis, was to speak mainly when interpreting associations (group associations), and otherwise remaining "abstinent" so as to avoid any "contamination" (Lichtenberg, Lachmann & Fossage, 2002). I have examined the drawbacks of this kind of legacy in my chapter on Freud (Chapter Six).

CHAPTER TWO

Taking position: what groups do we bring?

"Humankind has not woven the web of life. We are but one thread within it. Whatever we do to the web, we do to ourselves. All things are bound together. All things connect."

—Native American saying, 1854;
used in the recovery group below

This chapter introduces and applies ideas from two sources: (a) "positioning theory", and (b) the theory of "dialogical self". It is argued that these frameworks offer a rich understanding of the dynamics of human relationships, their (relative) fluidity, and how they are partially founded within everyday acts of conversation and lived exchange. Hence we "take" a position, we position others, are defined and defining within our interactions and discourses. When the self is envisaged as part of an emergent, dialogical process, rather than as self-enclosed property, we have a better way of comprehending our lives, including that witnessed in the therapy group. Wider social life is touched upon, involving the defining influence of history and of categories that carry enormous weight and embody discursive, and other forms of, power.

Let us start with two different traditions, and two forms of therapy. First, group analysis. In 1993, Liesel Hearst delivered a Foulkes lecture, "Our cultural cargo and its vicissitudes in group analysis" (Hearst, 1993). In literal terms cargo means goods, a consignment or haul, delivery, freight, baggage; in the metaphorical way in which Hearst uses the term, it refers to those symbolic possessions that we carry as part of being who we are, and that may be burdens, riches, or simply those goods that serve our needs. Through cross-cultural examples, she argues that "the small analytic group contains and discloses the historical and cultural self-component of its members" (op. cit., p. 391). The symbolic groups that we carry as individuals might include family, neighbourhood, social class, nation, and so forth. A kind of double outcome results from the work and process of therapy; a "unique individuality and communality emerge" (p. 403).

The second tradition is an interdisciplinary approach to psychotherapy associated with the "dialogical self" (Hermans, 2001; Hermans & Dimaggio, 2004a). This approach welds concepts of self from William James and G. H. Mead, amongst others, with concepts of the dialogical, as inspired by Bakhtin; in this way it can be said to be a blend of American pragmatism and Russian dialogism. Hermans (Hermans & Dimaggio, 2004a, p. 13) puts it this way: "The notion of the 'dialogical self' ... considers the self as a multiplicity of parts (voices, characters, positions) that have the potential of entertaining dialogical relationships with each other." Not only this, but he argues that, "[t]he self functions as a society, being at the same time part of the broader society on which the self participates" (op. cit., p. 13). The therapist seeks to trace the presence and emergence of such characters, each with their own distinctive voice, position, and story to be told, and to examine the power relations between them. Similarly, groups and cultures are located in the self as influential "collective voices". Hence, the usual starting point—How do individuals behave in a group?—can be reversed, and replaced with the question: How do groups behave within individuals? (Hermans, 2001; Turner, Hogg, Oakes, Reicher & Wetherell, 1987).

Two different traditions for sure, but each concurs with some general version of the notion that we are complex, multiple beings, always "off centre" as it were, and layered. We not only carry, but in a real sense are constituted by, our cultural and historical cargo, is the point that Hearst (1993) makes. And speaking discloses its presence. Roland

(2001, p. 320), makes the similar point that "dialogical theory can add to this important dimension of a historical layering of the self".

Positioning and dialogical self theory

I will concentrate on the theory of positioning as developed by Harré and colleagues (e.g., Harré & Van Langenhove, 1991) and that of the dialogical self as developed by Hermans and colleagues (e.g., Hermans & Hermans-Konopka, 2010). Even so, there can be no simple ownership of ideas here, as, for example, both these approaches acknowledge the influence of earlier feminist theory, which serves a powerful challenge to patriarchy and traditional positioning regarding the formation of gender, sexuality, inequalities, and so forth (Davies, 2000).[1]

Rom Harré: the discursive positioning of selves

Harré distinguishes position from earlier, sociological notions of role, so that whereas roles are relatively stable, formal, and long lasting, positions are more dynamic, even labile, and contestable. Put differently, positioning has more fluid connotations. In their broad outline, Davies and Harré (1999, p. 37) argue that positioning "is the discursive process whereby people are located in conversations as observably and subjectively coherent participants in jointly produced storylines. There can be interactive positioning in which what one person says positions another."

The diagram they use distinguishes (a) illocutionary force (related to speech act theory, as discussed in the preceding chapter), which refers to "admissible social acts" (i.e., the social significance of what is said and done), (b) positions, referring to assumed and ascribed rights and duties, and (c) story line(s), referring to the shaping of human interaction by narratives and accounts.

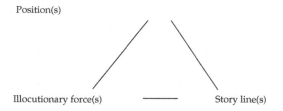

Subsequently, they suggest a fourth point, concerning the physical position and stances of the actors involved "(spaces"), such as a doctor standing and a patient lying down, an analyst behind a couch, a judge delivering a verdict to a defendant in the dock. In the case of groups it would include the circle of chairs.

As we will see in the historical examples below, certain social subjects and places associated to them can be classified and positioned as dangerous, aberrant, and undesirable—as in the "dangerous classes" of the nineteenth century. This also involved how such subjects were spoken about, and by whom, and the narratives developed about them. Even so, those so rendered develop counter-narratives, much against the odds, and, as Foucault (1979) observes, "Where there is power, there is resistance".

Harré and colleagues believe that selves arise within complicated "discursive practices", which include positions and positioning. Theirs is a compelling analysis that not only considers the creation and occupancy of positions, but examines how fruitful repositioning can be achieved. Positioning is a way in which personal agency and experience is defined and distributed, within networks of roles and relationships.

Hubert Hermans: the dialogical self

Although the language and theoretical provenance of Herman's work differs from that of Harré, there are some similarities and overlaps. Dialogical self is a theory and research paradigm that offers creative ways of understanding clinical and other domains. Dialogical self theory assumes that there are relationships *within* the space of self, varied voices and perspective points, and that how we speak, respond, and express our emotions involves a complex organised repertoire of positions. The self is not an enclosed sphere but, using the language of William James (e.g., the "I Self" and "Me Self"), has an extended social existence, at the very least—as in the notion of "my teacher", "my bank account", "my job", etc. We are "populated" by others throughout our lives and, using Baktin's imagery, we live a polyphonic life within networks, voices, and roles which change continually (Hermans, 2001). Although we move position as we travel through situations and life, we are easily tagged by our "positional history" (Hermans & Hermans-Konopka, 2010). Think only of the notion of reputation and how easily a person is placed by how they are received and remembered. The notion of self as open and decentred, however, amply allows ways of considering how change and self-innovation occurs, including through the dialogical space as provided by therapy. Here is how Hermans and Dimaggio (2004b, p. 2) summarise these overall points: "Given the intrinsic interwovenness of internal and external dialogues, the self does not function as a 'container' of cognition, thought and emotion, centralised in itself. It does not operate as a unified agency, in a multivoiced environment. Rather, the self is multivoiced because the multiplicity of voices is also in the self and their mutual relationships characterise the self as 'society of mind'". This has an important cultural dimension, in so far as we live in a world that is more variegated, more positionally complex than in former times.

In the examples that follow, two clinical, one historical, I aim to demonstrate the usefulness of such ideas.

Clinical example one

The burdened self

> The last few weeks I've had so many feeling from when I was small, so many small things which make me angry to think about. It's like with everything they always put drink first—like if we were on holiday, they would be in the pub all day, and we would have to play by ourselves, and if I was ill then that was a problem because they might be too hung-over to look after me. So I had to look after me. They were always in some kind of mood—loud when they were drunk, feeling sorry for themselves the day after, or guilty when they were off it—then I was given a lot of freedom, but kinda punished when they were back on it. Then there were all their so-called friends, the other boozers forever popping in. I didn't know if I was coming or going.
> [Barbara was nervous in her talking, glancing back and forth at me throughout].
> (Barbara, long-term member of an analytic group; for more on this example, see Weegmann, 2005a).

Barbara was in long-term recovery from her own addiction when she entered the group. Having changed her life around, through rehabilitation and Alcoholics Anonymous, she made further progress in the group. In the example, Barbara is reworking past experiences, looking back through grown-up eyes. Drinking was the norm in family life and as a child she had no means of "seeing it" for what it was at the time.

Not only this, but she had no sober parent, as both drank. There were dawning realisations growing up that her family was not "like others" and she felt awkwardness when friends wanted to visit (she put them off), or when the topic of family life was discussed at school (e.g., "Write about what you did on holiday"). In a succession of retrospective moments, she was able to re-evaluate her parents and family life. Using a metaphor from Heidegger (Inwood, 1997), one could say that the parental drinking could only be "unconcealed" once Barbara had created a "clearing" in her own mind and created stability through recovery; children adapt in implicit, sensori-motor modes to the worlds in which they live, from the start. Barbara was able to build a clearer description of family life, re-evaluating "lost time". Recovery and therapy, working together, gave her permission to narrate, to have a clear story to tell.

Barbara was effectively mourning aspects of her childhood. For example, noticing sequences of behaviour, such as: drinking parent—intoxicated parent—withdrawing/sick parent—dry parent. This was associated with affective cycles, such as: tension-disinhibition-moodiness-guilt. She felt anger and sadness, focused around the thought that "alcohol came first", and painful regret that she had done the same, during her drinking years. She used the art of vigilance, scanning her parents for indications of the state they were in and, above all, ensuring safety. Her nervous vigilance of me in the group was, I surmised, an expression of her need to maintain safety and to take note of my responses; the group's responses counted too, although her preoccupations with me as the "one in charge" had a particular salience. At first, Barbara experienced analytic group therapy as "too spontaneous" and worryingly free of "rules"; anxieties such as these were consistent with her experiences of a family life dominated by confusing priorities and inconsistent, if one likes, liquid rules. Reparation in such situations is made immeasurably difficult by the fact that parents with such difficulties not only deny but often cannot remember many of their actions, as a result of blackouts and so forth.

If one uses classic analytic ideas, it can be said that Barbara brought damaged internal figures, cargo, if one wills. Her communication can be seen as an effort at the reparation of herself and family as primary group. She had no concept of what a sober, predictable household was and perhaps the therapy group became an alternative psychosocial household within which new responses and understanding was build. In recognising damaged figures in such depth, her deprivations and the actual impact on her development and attachments could be addressed. But there is a wider cargo that she carries, that of the immersion by the family in a heavy drinking culture that goes beyond their own drinking.

Barbara was positioned to be the one who copes, the carer to ill parents, holding herself together in chaotic and absent situations (e.g., getting herself ready without help for school, or self-entertaining on holiday). Using dialogical self theory, one could postulate the formation of an inner "voice" that justifies her caring position as "that which needs to be done", "there is no alternative", etc. A more frightened, vulnerable self has to be suppressed in the face of such requirements. McDougall[2] (1986) talks of the dilemmas of the "cork child" whose psychic responsibility is one of managing a problematic parent(s), holding the plug on situations that could be even worse (e.g., through further intoxication, threats of violence, and so forth). Counter-phobic, and prematurely capable or caring, repertories are possible outcomes. On the other hand, in the recontextualisation that recovery and therapy provide, the voice of a vulnerable and neglected child does arise, quiet at first, perhaps, then more assertive, and so on. She can reposition herself as a suffering person who lost out and who has reasons for anger? This takes place "in dialogue" with other, adult self- positions—for example, being in recovery, being herself a mother, caring for others in the group versus receiving help, and so on—within the matrix created by other group members who will identify with, empathise, challenge, and so forth, from their varied positions. The deeper the dialogue, the richer, more expanded and populated, is the matrix (Weegmann, 2014a, for more on the concept of a "populated matrix"). Such voices have emotional and/or reasoned aspects, and the term dialogical in this context does not imply that such aspects are clear and neatly set out, indeed they are often sublingual (at first) and inchoate. Position repertoires can be considered in relation to a whole variety of issues—their accessibility, hierarchy, affective variety and flexibility (Hermans, 2004). It is in the very acts of exploration and response, in the performances of speech (Baktin refers to "addressivity"), that new voices are strengthened and gain narrative credence.[3]

Recovery (in this case, from substance misuse) is itself a position of change, an attainment, as in the recovery of a "sober self". In this example, rehabilitation at first, then Alcoholics Anonymous, then the group, provided successive discursive spaces in which articulations of past and present could be worked upon. O'Halloran (2008) describes a compound of interactive and reflective positioning; "Recovering, not recovered" is how AA puts it, placing the emphasis on a process rather than event (see below, and Chapter Five). Recovery can be regarded in part as a better dialogue, or conversation between parts of the self, which assists forward development (Weegmann, 2005b). People find a confident, sober voice. Group analysis, with its conventions and extended conversations, creates new opportunities for elaboration of self, voice, and the rehearsing of alternatives. In his model, Hermans (2006), quite separately from any psychoanalytic tradition, uses the useful metaphor of self as a "theatre of voices". Hopefully, increased positional flexibility results, so that people can renegotiate their experiences and lives.

Clinical example two

Some discussion of the wider context of recovery is required before I discuss the recovery group in question.

The precursors of the modern recovery movement in mental health are many and varied, including anti-psychiatry, consumer/survivor networks, authority given to "lived experience", and the empowering influence of other "new social movements" (feminist, gay/lesbian, disability rights). Without wishing to engage in debates about the radical versus ameliorative status of the recovery movements (as though these were strict alternatives), I will accept it on its own terms, as articulated in the form with which I am most familiar, and trained (Perkins & Rinaldi, 2007; Repper & Perkins, 2003; for a useful review of the wide diversity of modern recovery perspectives, see Carson, McManus & Chander, 2010). It is argued that this movement illustrates well the role of social positioning and individual change, contesting as it does the definitional power of psychiatry and the authority of social institutions, creating new spaces of empowerment for those who feel the opposite, disempowered. To orient ourselves, let us enumerate some general principles about the recovery model.

- Traditionally, mental health conditions are seen only as a clinical challenge, requiring diagnosis, care, treatment, containment, etc.
- By contrast, recovery approaches regard mental health conditions as pre-eminently a social and personal challenge.

• Recovery emphasises possibility over psychopathology, potential over deficit and dysfunction. It avoids a language of pathology.
• Recovery is concerned with the rebuilding of lives and seeks to find meaning in what has happened, not just symptoms for removal.
• Recovery aims at helping individuals to grow within and beyond crisis, and beyond what has happened in the past, without denying it.
• Recovery emphasises lived experience and the construction of personal narratives.
• Hope, control, and opportunity are central.
• Its wider goal is equal citizenship for people with mental health conditions.

In a corrective to accusations of utopianism, Repper and Perkins (2003, p. ix) underline that "[r]ecovery is not about 'getting rid' of problems. It is about seeing people beyond their problems—abilities, possibilities, interests and dreams—and recovering the social roles and relationships that give life value and meaning."

Like any cultural counter-position, the recovery movement makes sense in relation to that which it is countering or tempering. Using Laclau's (1996) language, it is an articulation that seeks to distinguish itself, although, as Perkins is all too aware, such movements are easily pulled back into the domain of traditional psychiatry and rationalisation ("everyone believes in recovery now"; recovery principles, it is claimed, are incorporated into all modern mental health services). So the extent to which the movement might be re-coupled by that from which it seeks to distinguish itself, remains an open question.

Although the group to be discussed was professionally initiated (as a new group, by the author), the aim was to sow seeds of more independent user involvement and to establish more recovery-oriented practice into ward life.

"My recovery" group

A weekly group was set up on an acute psychiatric ward, entitled, "My recovery". Through a number of semi-structured exercises, the group encouraged maximum participation around recovery principles. In terms of framework, the group was open to all patients who were willing to attend (the average was six). No one was excluded, the criteria being: anyone and everyone is welcome who is able to sit and take part in a group. Once in the group, if patients were uncomfortable or distracted to the point of leaving (very common), they were encouraged to try to settle and stay, with group help, or given permission to take a short rest and rejoin quickly if they felt able. Diagnosis was deemed non-relevant and patients could attend at any stage during their stay, and to attend every week if they were on the ward any length of time. The immediate challenges were (a) creating a group presence, so as to increase ward focus on recovery, (b) creating such a group culture within a transitory setting, with rapid turn-over of members, and frequent ward crises, and (c) building an effective, meaningful experience in a "one-session group", whilst varying the content so as to remain engaging and stimulating for those attending several times (Yalom, 1983, pioneered the concept of the "single session time frame group" for in-patient settings). A delicate balance was struck between exploring the particularities of patient experience and more universal themes of recovery, that is, how does *anyone* undergoing distressing and disturbing experiences sort themselves out, build hope and gain trust in a process of change, however fleeting or elusive that might feel at the time? Critically, the group promoted maximum exchange and support between members, many of whom were anxious and unsettled in groups. In a memorable example of intuitive mirroring, one member, who appeared "thought disordered" when talking about herself (like all psychiatric terminology, there is not only a wide range of ways of referring to the allegedly same phenomenon, but what is considered "disorganised" is a relative question (Rule, 2005)), demonstrated remarkable clarity—and empathy—("thought order"?) in encouraging her reticent peer, who was nervous in talking.

Group convention, each time, involved (a) welcomes, (b) first-name introductions, with a varying related task (e.g., "Tell us your first name and a favourite animal"), (c) brief introduction to the concept of recovery and wellbeing, and, (d), a participatory, creative exercise, with materials provided (e.g., "Draw an image, picture, or symbol to express what recovery means to you"; "Draw an image or write some keywords that express your most important values"; "Identify with some of the keywords provided"—I had a stock of simple laminated images and words, also added to by previous groups; "Look at these recovery sayings and poems"—I had a collection which was placed on the floor, and added to, as above—"and see which ones apply to you", or, "Write your own that can act as reminders in your own journey of recovery", etc.). The exercise was done in silence (five or ten minutes) and everyone was invited to share what they had done or found interesting. The group concluded with an invitation (in turn) to say how each person had found the experience and what they had received. I took part in the exercises and sharing, and other staff were expected to do likewise; this meant a degree of personal disclosure, for example, regarding a difficult moment in our lives, and activities to which we turn as part of our wellbeing. Encouragement of reflective conversation was considered critical, a conversation not dominated by the psychologist's theory or view of problems, and so forth (see Hermans, 2003).

The group did gain increased presence in ward life and trialled an outside "expert by experience" guest to the group (an ex-patient). Plans were underway to invite other ex-clients and to create a group portfolio/mural from their materials, as consented to.

Comment

The discourses of the handover, ward round, case conference, and so on, are saturated with reference to symptom and dysfunction, questions of management, plan, and risk. In such discussions, it is interesting to speculate on those enunciative rights concerning "who speaks, in what way, about whom and what", and how these relate to the dynamics of consultant, medical, and nursing hierarchies and, of course, that of patient/staff . To use the language of Harré, people express themselves broadly in alignment with the rights, duties, and positions as required by a given social order (in this case an inpatient ward). On the staff side there will be inevitable differentiations, so that, for example, occupational therapists and psychologist have a different way of contributing—sometimes in marked contrast with, or at least "as well as"—to the discourses of medicine, reflecting their different positions within the framework of care. Where patients are present (ward rounds, etc.), their contribution is elicited in particular ways (e.g., active questioning), with the focus on presenting problems, risks, medication, and aftercare plans. The sociological notion of "footing" is useful, concerning as it does the social presentation, position, and alignment of individuals to each other (Goffman, 1981).[4] So, on what "footing" do the different participants speak? Professionals occupy positions and exercise particular speech rights within their practices, whereas clients are by definition "ill people", at least to start with, and as such are on a much more vulnerable, dependent footing.

Of course the group was, by definition, a therapeutic activity, as distinct from these other forums of decision-making and review. And although professionally organised (as it was a new group), the aim was to bring more emphasis on the voice and experiences of the members. Our approach was to encourage patients to be consultants to their experience and to talk about their qualities and strengths as well as their worries. As a recovery-oriented group, the discussion was not so much problem-focused as centred upon personal pathways to recovery, values and life horizons. Lewis (2012) refers to the strengths-based and non-linear aspects of recovery practice, also to the role of creative expression in helping people to refind and build upon such strengths. The emphasis of recovery practice is quite the opposite to the problem-focused perspective of (traditional) group therapy and analysis. Recovery practice offers an alternative position for patients as individuals, beginning a process through which they might begin to take back control within their lives. And, in wider, more social terms, recovery practice suggests positions within which dignity and equality (and its opposites) are addressed. It is a form of "meaning-based practice", within which such positions and narratives are forged.

Recovery is a value which seeks to promote a more equal sense of participation and citizenship, against considerable odds. Mental illness is an invalidating experience, in so many ways. Another aspect of recovery is providing space in which definitions of normality and standards of social and self-expectation can be contested. We know, for example, that stigma towards those with mental illness is a considerable challenge, however much progress has been made. In Goffman's (1963, p. 3) classic definition, stigma concerns "an attribute that is deeply discrediting", the recognition of which reduces the stigmatised person "from a whole and usual person to a tainted, discounted one", hence his notion of "spoiled identity". Since self-stigma (or "internalised discrimination") is disabling, as is external stigma, recovery practice helps people to better locate what they are carrying, and to build new narratives of personhood, meanwhile challenging the mental health system, indeed society at large, to examine its ready assumptions regarding others (Brohan, Gauci, Sartorius & Thornicroft, 2010).

Positioning: an example from history

"Dangerous classes" and "lower sorts"

In the Britain of the past, there were many of ways of referring to, and creating differences, within society, such as "orders", "rank", "sorts", "stations", and so forth. Tudor society had its clergy, chivalry (lay elite), and commonalty (everyone else). In the nineteenth century, Dickens (1844) summed up this penchant for order in his catchy saying, "O let us love our occupations, Bless the squire and his relations, Live upon our daily rations, And always know our proper stations". France had its versions, with estates, privilégiés (e.g., nobles, clergy), and roturiers (commoners) (Rudé, 1995). These depict positions within hierarchies, with associated estimations of contribution and worth, assumed to reflect a natural state of affairs. In nineteenth-century discourses addressing issues of pauperism, its faces (e.g., ruffians, vagabonds, dregs, destructive classes, etc.) and places (e.g., slums, rookies, dark quarters, etc.), commentators articulated a variety of common fears and concern. One noted social reformer, Reverend Henry Solly,[5] contrasting different sorts of populations, observed "how different a London mob is from a docile agricultural peasantry or orderly Lancashire operatives", whilst poet and critic Matthew Arnold,[6] warned of the rise of the common "Populace", as "vast residuum … marching where it likes, meeting where it likes, bawling what it likes, breaking what it likes" (both quotations in Stedman Jones, 2013, p. 243).

Views such as these were neither rare nor abstract, but deeply influential and embedded in social debate, policy, and administrations of reform. In terms of positioning theory they implicate a number of denigrated "subject positions", although the subject in this sense does not refer to individuals as such but to social agents. In a real sense, such "positions" were features of "the local moral landscape" (Harré, Moghaddam, Pilkerton Cairnie, Rothbart & Sabat, 2009, p. 9), each associated with attendant rights, duties, for example, expectation of showing deference, not seen, and so forth. The agents in question are often subdivided, as in the case of the poor who might be characterised by other distinctions, such as vagrants, beggars, clever paupers, honest poor, respectable working classes, and so on. Hence social reformer Henry Solly, distinguishes the feared urban mob from the supposedly dependable, docile rural worker or peasant. Radicals too also made distinctions, as in Marx's term for depicting a degenerative element, the *lumpenproletariat* (from the German, "miscreant" or even "rag"). Social positioning entails comparisons and rhetorical grounding, as in expressions such as "lower destructive class", "drama of low life", a "common sink", as well as in the influential "levelling up" theories that promoted housing reforms (i.e., that slum clearance and rebuilding would encourage industrious, honest workers, in a benign circle of improvement). Positions, as relational markers, make sense within what Foucault describes as a constellation of discourses, power, and knowledge (*"pouvoir-savoir"*; Foucault, 1975) and, in these examples, involved conditions, for some (paupers), of almost absolute powerlessness, with neither voice nor resources (although they would of course have their own codes, street argot, songs, ability to raise reactions, and so forth; by definition, we know little about how paupers described themselves compared to how they were described by their educated "betters"). Moral positioning and paternalism is powerfully implicated and applied across the political spectrum in the nineteenth century, albeit it with important differences, including socialist discourses, and the secular, and of course the religious. As for the latter, the nineteenth-century evangelist movement was influential in the formation of middle-class morality, including what historians call the "cult of conduct", with its gospel of duty, the primacy of work, sanctity of home and family, and so on (Bradley, 2006). Many of their charitable and missionary efforts were based upon a "war on vice" and a quest to convert the nation and the poor. Further, in extended acts of global, imperial positioning, missionary societies sought out the "heathen" multitudes oversees with their civilising projects and missions. The radical movements of the earlier nineteenth century, such as Chartism, attempted to reposition and dignify the (respectable) working classes, as, in some Christian discourses, equivalent to "Christ's poor", there to be "raised" (the height and position metaphor again) by God (Thompson, 1980).

Certain social subjects and places associated to them were classified and positioned as dangerous, aberrant, and undesirable, moreover adversely positioned with respect to other poor counterparts, who were seen as more reliable or sturdy, such as the compliant rural labourer or deserving poor. In the discourses of description alluded to, those doing the describing were authorities, politicians, policy makers, and philanthropists, licensed to speak, pass judgement, and classify, or writers with an established "voice". Their words counted, had legitimacy, whereas those of the "dangerous classes" did not. In terms of story lines, discourses concerning this sector of the urban poor were woven into complex accounts of human evolution and degeneracy, stories of darkness and the spiritual condition of society, or, in the different discourse of Marxism, seen as a subpopulation who might detract from the class struggle, and so on. The relationship between the classes was a major issue at stake, although for liberals, conservatives, and most radicals alike, this grouping or subclass was also defined in terms of the imagery of the "masses" and the "mob" (Briggs, 1985). Racial attributions were often added to the dangerous mix, as in instances of anti-Irish and other anti-immigrant sentiment regarding the poor. This is not to say that the "triangle" of definition in such cases was entirely fixed, as movement still took place. And, even in conditions of abjection and powerlessness, the poor might, and did, refuse their allocated place, by remonstration, riot, even the cultivation of blasphemy in everyday speech as a form of curse or irreverence. Indeed, swearing and cursing have been used throughout history by the less powerful to have an impact on the powerful.

Conclusion

We adopt positions throughout our lives, and are equally invited, even pressed, into positions by others, through all the practices and groups in which we find ourselves. The self can usefully be envisaged as a theatre of positions from which we act out a complex psychic repertory; we "carry" and are "staged" by a cultural and historical cargo. Not only this, but whole social categories, such as classes and social groups, are also positioned in complicated ways, given or denied rights, allowed or disallowed speech, to put it crudely.

This chapter has explored theories of positioning and the dialogical self and how these help us develop an in-depth and in-breadth analysis of the therapeutic group, as well as wider formation of groups and classes within society.

Notes

1. Two feminist writers to note, are (a) psychologist, Wendy Holloway (1984), who looks at how female and male subjects are subtly positioned in numerous discourses, and (b) poet and writer, Adrianne Rich

(Yorke, 1997), who developed an innovative analysis of the complex positioning and locations of subjectivity, gender and sexuality (I am grateful to Rachel Cohen, personal communication, for drawing my attention to such feminist scholarship).

2. The late Joyce McDougall, who was a French-based analyst, offers a novel, "independent" (but not in the British psychoanalytic sense, as it incorporates French and Kohutian insights) synthesis of psychoanalysis. Not only this, but her imagery and metaphors have parallels with dialogical self theory: "Psychoanalysis is a theatre on whose stage all our psychic repertory may be played. In these scenarios the features of the internal characters undergo many changes, the dialogues are rewritten and the roles recast ... accounts are settled" (McDougall, 1986, p. 284).

3. In an interesting note, Hermans and Hermans-Konopka (2010, p. 253) contrast dialogical and narrative psychology. Although certainly different in emphasis, as they clearly argue, my approach seeks to transcend these distinctions, making optimal use of the value of both approaches; narrative psychology benefits from the notion of dynamic, dialogical positions and dialogical psychology in turn benefits from an emphasis on how lives are subject to narrative expression and definition.

4. Goffman uses many valuable terms that have spatial, positional connotations, such as frame, alignment, footing, and regions to capture subtle and more deliberate changes in speech and social interaction, some of which are explored in the preceding chapter. Footing in particular refers to a participants' stance, posture and projected self—how they wish to "come across".

5. The Reverend Henry Solly was a noted social reformer and campaigner for charity organisations, working men's clubs, and garden cities. Inspired by the reformist cause, he became a Chartist, the working class movement for political reform in the mid-nineteenth century.

6. Matthew Arnold was a poet and social critic, a "sage writer" skilled at chastising and instructing his readers on the social issues of the day. He speculated on the social classes and their possible degenerations. With characteristic frankness Arnold summarily described the three social groups as "an upper class materialized, a middle class vulgarized, and a lower class brutalized" (Arnold, 1888, p. 188).

CHAPTER THREE

Remembering monsters

"Then was this island—
Save for the son that she did not litter here,
A freckled whelp hag-born—not honour'd with
A human shape."

—Shakespeare, *The Tempest* (I. ii. 281–284)

T his chapter is a cultural exploration of the monster, and its successor figures, such as the savage and freak. It covers four examples: (a) medieval anti-Semitic imagery, as based on the backdrop of the medieval monster; (b) the exotic monsters and savages of the New World; (c) the literary monster as imagined by Mary Shelley in *Frankenstein*; and (d) new uses of deformity as illustrated by the nineteenth-century freak show. I speculate on the roles that monsters play within human relations, their defining and disturbing potential. Monsters mirror something of how humans envisage and construct preferred identities at a human and group level, although cannot be reduced as mere projections of ourselves, as they too (however imaginary there are) influence who we are.

Wherever human beings are, there too are monsters. And wherever human beings have been, or might (still) go, there monsters already are, from the New World to outer space. Somehow we need them—as intimate strangers, as familiar unfamiliars. History is over-populated by monsters—barbarians, Amazons, giants, cyclopes, sciapods, Gog and Magog, Satan, demons, heretics, witches, cynocephali, dragons, blemmyae, werewolves, ghosts, mermaids, gargoyles, Grendel, savages, fiends, brutes, freaks, mobs, living curiosities, Frankenstein, nondescripts, pinheads, psychos, zombies, Daleks, Vulcans, Hyrule warriors, Slenderman, Moshi monsters, extreme bodies, and armies of others too numerous to name. They might populate entire lands, as in Greek and medieval concepts of the "Marvels of the East" (India), and were sited at the margins of maps, manuscripts, the unknown world; in border regions, borderlands (Walsh, 2006; Weegmann, 2008). But, more worrying still, they could inhabit our spaces and interiors, infiltrating communities and worming their influence, as in the case of the devil's pact with the witch. Shakespeare's extras include all manner of ghosts, spirits, witches and "human" monsters; Richard III famously depicts himself "Deform'd, unfinish'd, sent before my time/Into this breathing world, scarce half made up".[1] In R. L. Stevenson's (1979) nineteenth-century novella, words are insufficient to the job of describing the elusive Mr. Hyde, who is called, variously: thing, ugly, pale, dwarfish, troglodytic, creature, and ape (Weegmann, 2014a). Inherently disturbing and disrupting, our reactions to them vary, from fear and loathing, fascination and awe, incredulity and amusement, rejection and pity, horror and curiosity. Likewise what we do with them varies, whether it be slaying, being warned, discovering, imprisoning, segregating, photographing, or administering treatment. St. Augustine's (1958) *City of God*, written in the late Roman period, was intended to console Christians as to the eventual triumph of their faith, and claimed that the existence of monsters is paradoxical, as they are teachers, portents, and reminders (from *monstrare*, to demonstrate, *monere*, to warn). They are examples of sin, instances of error, and, later, sites of pathology, and might have connections with the supernatural. There is an aesthetics of horror and a cultural use of the grotesque in the way in which monsters are depicted in art and literature, inspiring rhetoric to great effect, as in the following medieval description of demons: "terrible in shape with great heads, long necks, thin faces, yellow complexions, filthy beards, shaggy ears, wild foreheads, fierce eyes, foul mouths, horses' teeth, throats vomiting flames, twisted jaws, thick lips, strident voices, singled hair, fat cheeks, pigeon breasts, scabby thighs … they grew so terrible to hear with their mighty shriekings that they filled almost the whole intervening space between earth and heaven with their discord-ant bellowing" (quoted in Higgs Strickland, 2000, p. 50; on the concept of grotesque, see Edwards & Graulund, 2013). So, whether at the level of imagination, myth, belief, or artistic representation, it seems we owe monsters a considerable debt of gratitude. Feared as they might be, or laughed at and pilloried as "jokes of nature" (Aristotle's *lusus naturae*), some would say that they have the last laugh; "The monster always escapes", as Cohen (1997) puts it.

How humans figure themselves, and the monsters that surround them, is a challenge to social theory. Strictly speaking, equivalence is not quite apposite, since the question is not one of like-to-like, human-to-human comparison. Of course, with idea of "human monsters", the situation is more complicated, as in the case of the freak, whose oddity and deformity was not so much monsterised as held up as grotesque and incongruous, for the freak "undoes form" (Edwards & Graulund, 2013, p. 86). There are, it would seem, many ways of seeing monsters and monstrosity, of imagining their existence, which defies any sin-gle or simple explanation. Besides, authors at different periods could and did hold divergent views and representations of monstrosity are incredibly varied, with some, even, portrayed as protective and hospi-table, even if their external form was troubling, such as the Golem in Jewish folklore, the Arimaspians of the East and the humble werewolf (which is no longer associated with kind traits, but the opposite) of early French literature, Bisclavret. In many ways then they echo what Foucault (1977, p. 35) says about the complicated nature of transgres-sion, in so far as they are manifest in codependent plays of transgres-sion and limit, with the former not related to the latter as "black to white, the prohibited to the lawful, the outside to the inside … Rather their relationship takes the form of a spiral which no simple infrac-tion could exhaust". Further, building on a suggestion explored by Williams (1999) in his study of medieval monsters (teratology), it is suggested that monster/human relationships can be understood in terms of a kind of negation (*via negativia*), in so far as the mystery of the monster tells us something about what we, as humans, are *not*. The same applies to those human kinds marked under a negative term, by their oddity; in other words, those human beings distinguished by deformity reassure the human beings not so marked of their normalcy and integrity. Still, they are close at hand, even inside us, indeed we may turn into beasts, as the example of *Jekyll and Hyde* demonstrates. This distance and proximity, safe or otherwise, is a critical if not defining feature of the monster.

Medieval monsters

Human, animals ("mere brutes") and monsters were strictly separate types of being, but whilst such separation was critical to medieval classifications, there were inevitable grey areas and anomalies, such as the werewolves (*lycanthropus*) who changed forms, and crossovers, as evidenced in many human-animal hybrids, such as the dog-headed men of the East (*cynocephali*), or, in his observations of "Irish races" by Gerald of Wales (1951), the half-ox half-man, held up as an example of a nefarious union. Indeed, it can be argued that with the onset of the Middle Ages, the presence of more ambivalent figures, less separated, as it were, living alongside and within communities, made the monster a much more pressing threat to moral order; "the monster's very existence is a rebuke to boundary and closure" (Cohen, 1996, p. 7). Indeed, it was their odd, intimate connection that made them more of a mortal danger, particularly those monsterised human groups and bands, such as heretics, Saracens, lepers, prostitutes, and others. Not everywhere, at all times, or in a uniform manner, but with a certain convergence and consistency of logic nevertheless. Monsters are not created out of nothing, but are reworked products, and given new combinations and reiterations, are guaranteed long life. Said (1978) argues that novelty and familiarity are controlled and that "a new median category emerges, a category that allows one to see new things, things seen for the first time, as versions of a previously known thing" (p. 58). Arguably, the threat posed by the extensive changes of the early medieval period increased the necessity of control, both at a practical and theological level; at the very least, account had to be made of it (Bynum, 1995). For, as Bynum argues, if the old England (pre-Norman) was seen as stable and unchanging, at least in imaginary, retrospective reckoning, major movements and devastations forced new accounts of life, movements such as the Crusades and the utter devastations to population caused by the Black Death[2] (in England, 1348–50), as well as the frailty of life in more general terms. Things were not always what they seemed and within a given place and time, a range of malevolent figures could arise, of which we shall consider one.

"Hateful to crist and to his compaignye"[3]*: Jews*

The reasons why the Middle Ages saw increasing persecution of various groups is a large question and suffice to say here that by the end of the first millennium, with the consolidation of Papal and ecclesiastical power and interests of feudal and monarchical rulers, there was a redefinition of Christendom, including its orthodoxy and enemies. In this respect, the Great Schism of 1378, splitting Papal power, was also critical. The period saw the formation of a compelling "external Other", whose presence coincided with geographical distance (e.g., the threat from the East) and proximity, on the borders of Christianity. Western Christendom (or the Kingdom of God or Christian Republic) increasingly identified this threat from the East, from the enemies of Christianity, variously described as the "heathen", "Saracen", "infidel". Satan had a new, terrifyingly active presence in the world and, alongside the external, Islamic Other, there was a search to identify and root out the "Other within", the "demonic hosts" as Cohn (1967, p. 16) graphically describes them. In his illuminating examination of the birth of medieval demonology, Boureau (2006) talks about a new cartography of fear, indeed obsession, with this no ordinary evil. Theologians grappled with the fact of the apparent proximity and sheer density of demons and the relative permeability of human beings to their influence, as well as to its opposite, angelic influence. Although not entirely reducible to heresy, what was the position of Jews within these new, potential criminal zones?

The reasons are over-determined, but Jews in Western (particularly Northern) Europe had an increasingly precarious position, an ambivalent and multivalent existence (Bale, 2006). In spite of its Judaic origins and continuities with the Old Testament, Christianity came to regard Jews in contradictory ways, both as a remnant, reminder religion, indeed often valued as such—not to mention as helpful if dependent economic communities—whilst also a source of trouble and corrupting influence within the Christian body/politic. In complex associations with earlier myths and emergent fears, the Jew was easily identified as demon, sorcerer, and heretic. There was a need for increasingly sharp differentiations within medieval Christianity (the infamous Fourth Lateran Council in 1215 ordered Jews and Muslims to wear distinctive clothes or badges to avoid confusion with Christians; it also forbad the formation of new religious orders, reflecting an obsession with heresy, lest confusion reigned, as part of its collective identity, resulting in the definition of more and more dangerous elements. Gilmore (1993, p. 19), using the anthropology of Edmund Leach (1982, p. 4), talks of "abnormalities that fall into the cracks of belief systems". The "narrative assault" on Jews had begun (Rubin, 1999).

Narrative partitioning (Murray, 1995) involves the discursive production, through images as much as texts, of monsters and the foregrounding of their difference. Partitioning involves a work of separation, dividing up, keeping apart. Experts in early modern Jewish history have analysed the changing languages of orthodoxy and its disturbance in the medieval period, with new polarities, as in the figure of "the Jew" as inferior being and antithesis of "the Christian". Strident rhetoric and new tropes arose, new dangers named. Narrative partitioning subsumed images of Jews, who were increasingly accused of committing monstrous or perfidious acts (Higgs Strickland, 2000). The myths attributed to Jews were reworkings of ancient beliefs and were beliefs that also attached to other groups, particularly "Christian" heretics. These myths, including ritualised blood libels, host desecration and poisonings, coin clipping, and so on, gained a powerful currency, striking, as they were seen to, at the very body of Christ/Church—Christ's dignity contrasting with Jewish cruelty, Christian integrity contrasting the perfidy of Jews. The earliest English accusation of ritual murder was in 1144 when a boy, William of Norwich, was alleged to have been sacrificed; he was subsequently venerated by Christians as a saint, and a popular cult followed. As with this, other accusations and falsehoods were woven into a fast accumulating narrative, and, oft repeated (the last case in England being Hugh of Lincoln in 1255), they were presented as fact. In this regard, Langmuir (1990) refers to the formation of increasingly "chimerical" stereotypes. We do not know how much such representations affected the general populace, as distinct from the educated elite, but, as built into narratives, ballads, manuscripts, and reproduced in art and woodcuts, and so on, they became *exempla* through which dominant versions of events gained credence. Bale (2010) considers images of the Passion within the Salvin Hours, a lavish medieval English manuscript, in particular the presence of ugly, grotesque stereotypes of Jews, often in profile form.[4] Amongst other techniques, the animalisation of human groups places them in a "lower" category of existence and so often is used to justify violence. The medieval world equated Christianity with beauty and Judaism with ugliness, inventing modes of ideal, devotional comportment, based on Christ's (and/or saintly) grace and clemency. In this respect, art historian Higgs Strickland (2010, p. 3) points out that "word and picture are equal bearers of monstrosity", with, in the case of Jews, external appearance aligned with moral depravity. Having certain groups seen as attacking the very core of Christianity, such as Christ's passion and the host, struck terror into people and served as warning.

Bale (op. cit., p. 57) notes the importance to culture of "memory work", of "[t]hings felt, things remembered and repeated, things believed and things perceived …", which was disastrous to many Jews. Human groups conceive themselves within aesthetic registers, forms in which they recognise themselves, in a cloth of interwoven narrative constructions. Medieval Christendom in this sense offers a fascinating illustration of what sociologists call "symbolic monopoly", and not just symbolic in matters of open heresy. Segregations, both physical and conceptual, could enable peaceful coexistence, but also raise the spectre of contamination. Segregated places can become criminal spaces, within the logic of a malign, psychic geography. As Berger and Luckmann put it (1966, p. 140), "[t]he trouble begins whenever the 'strangeness' is broken through, and the deviant universe appears as a possible habitat for one's own people." The Jews were expelled from England in 1290— and no doubt some crept back, undisclosed—but nevertheless left a "spectral presence" within culture, in which their image continued to exist within the categories of "familiarity" (Ara Krummel, 2011; Kruger, 2005).

A central aspect of such cultural "memory work" is a fixing of associations in the collective imagination and the juxtaposition of different elements. Elsewhere, I have addressed this in terms of a veritable constellation of dangers, an "exclusionary matrix" (Weegmann, 2014a). In the case of Jews, who were already expected to demonstrate "honourable dependence" on royal power, they were easily associated with blood, deformed features, sinful behaviour, which, importantly, might also be displayed by the Christian (demonstrating "Jewish behaviour"; Bildhauer, 2003). The Jew hovered under a negative sign, symbolically connected to other marked figures, such as Cain, whose function was as reminder;[5] in disputations (formalised debates, sometime forced upon others by Christian prelates, itself a word derived from *prælatus*, to "set above or over"), Jews were often presented as obstinate or accused, in the words of one French Saint, of "inveterate Obduracy" (Moore, 2014).

Such juxtaposing, with similar and different elements combined, many of them exotic (especially on the Continent), was clear in the demonisation of heresy traced by Cohn (1975), and, following the medieval period, by the witches, with their pacts, Sabbaths, and their other manifold devilments.

"Presently they saw naked people"[6]: old worlds/new worlds

Pagden (1982) suggests that before 1492, the margins and unknowns of the world were "imaginary spaces" filled by Europeans with the natural phenomena of ancient and medieval literature. But the Plinian pantheon of creatures moved from the East and Africa to be relocated in the New World, which became the new canvas of human imagination. Nature, climate, and anthropology figured as inseparable wholes in this landscape of strange fauna, satyrs, pygmies, cannibals, Amazons, mermaids, wild men, dog-headed men. Woven into the gallery was a complex Christian mythology of the world and its origins, based on the Book of Genesis, subsequent fall from grace and degeneracy, even the notion that the different sons of Noah helped produce fabulous beings in different spheres of the world (Higgs Strickland, 2012).

The link between land, vegetation, and the man/animal kingdom is interesting to explore in the light of how these Other world(s) were seen. A famous engraving (1575) by Jan van der Straet allegorises the new continent of America as a woman, overlooked by Amerigo Vespucci (an explorer, after whom the Americas were named) holding the Christian flag and, in the background, various associated paraphernalia of parrots, tapirs, bows and arrows, cannibal feasts. Vespucci is the dominant, standing figure, whilst the reclining, submissive woman receives the gifts he symbolically bestows; at once the new continent is legitimised, Christianised, and possessed. An act of grace more than one of conquest. The background represents a view of American lands, with its strange animals, lyrical landscape, primitive peoples, and savagery. Other lands are potential, virgin territory. Continually, in descriptions and representations of these early encounters with the New World, there is allegorisation, with a fine line between the possibility of discovering an early paradise, a prelapsarian state of man, or, instead, a ferocity and savagery of lands long occluded (Hulme, 1984; also Hulme's 1986 analysis of the Spanish construction of the Caribbean and "Hispaniola" and its fascination with cannibals). In terms of their reception, Spanish representations in pictures, log books, writings, and reports wavered between idealised tributes from grateful Indians to fierce clashes with warlike adversaries. Columbus, a deeply religious man, believed in the existence of an earthly paradise, located in the temperate regions beyond the equator, and his references to "Indians" links them closely with nature and animals. This was consistent with the European idea of the chain of being and hierarchy of the world, with Indians fitted somewhere between birds and trees. Columbus's first reference to the sight of Indians is noteworthy: "presently they saw naked people", which relates to a theme of spiritual as much as actual nudity. Moreover, said to be virgin of any religion ("without a creed"), Indians were regarded as naturally predisposed to Christianity (Todorov, 1984). The bringer and bearer is the agent of interpellation, the one who bestows knowledge or truth, and who brings the right religion.

Although the natural world and the world of man were linked closely together in such discourses of discovery, the greatest shock for Europeans was undoubtedly the encounter with human diversity, and there was some disappointment that the more fantastic monsters had not been encountered. Yet within this diversity, monstrosity of another kind could be found. Smith (1997) writes: "What gripped the European imagination was the social otherness of native peoples" (p. 97). The image of the barbarian is an old one, established in some detail by the Greeks for whom *barbarkos* originally meant a blabber, marked by an inability to speak Greek and also the inability to form civil societies, typified by the city; "[b]eyond the city, as Aristotle had said ... there were only beasts and heroes" (Pagden, 1993, p. 2). The story of how Christians reoccupied this image and endowed it with new meanings, with pagans as outsiders, is well known, so that the *communitas christianae* replaced the Greek *oikumene*. According to Aquinas, pagans were either "invincibly ignorant", not having heard the Gospel, through no fault of their own, or were "vincibly ignorant"—groups such as Jews and Muslims, who had refused to listen and take heed of the Word. The Indians were part of a pagan world, but fell under the category of the "invincibly ignorant". One way out of the impasse of justifying the bounds of temporal power was to return to classical ideas, including Aristotelean ideas of others, the barbarians and Indians, as "nature's slaves". Columbus saw himself and was seen by his followers, such as La Casas, as a representative of the *Orbis Christianus*, the bringer of light. Some suggest that Columbus distinguished the monstrous and the marvellous and was in fact sceptical about the presence of the former, at least in its more exotic variants (Barnum, 2012). His mission drew on crusade metaphors, with the idea of world travel signifying a final phase of world conversion, including the conversion of the Chinese (he believed he had landed in Asia) and the final elimination of Islam. We must not forget that with expansion and discovery came an early form of globalisation and, indeed, eventually of seeing the world as a "whole" (the earliest example of a three-dimensional globe, as distinct from the two-dimensional map, is 1492).

Expansion and conquest created classificatory and epistemological dilemmas. How would the new world be placed within the certainties and framework of the old? Initially, the new others were responded to almost entirely within the assumptive world of Europeans and Christianity—the "gaze of the European [is] the only one which could confer existence upon the world" (Pagden, 1993, p. 7). Yet, in spite of this, there was also a trend of scepticism that raised troubling moral questions. How were new peoples to be conceptualised within a Christian theology of descent and assumptions of mankind's uniformity? On the one hand, there was the Adamite version of origin and the integrity of mankind. On the other, how could one understand a world of occluded peoples, living, as Las Casas said, behind the "locked doors of the ocean sea"? How did they survive the Biblical Flood? Were these really human beings or was there something "not quite" human being about them? One theory, albeit heretical, was that of human *discontinuity*, the theory that Indians fitted in differently to the chain of being. There may have been a "second Adam", spontaneously created at a later stage in human history, or, perhaps, Indians were descended from insects and other "natural" beings, rather than from man. A further idea and image, evoked by Columbus, was the idea of the "other within the other", the idea of subcategories of animal-like, savage beings, "wild men" who lived at the margins of human society, always there, always over the hill or on the next island, even if never quite discovered. In many ways this was a reworking of a familiar category within a new context, that of the woodwose or wild man. White's (1972) classic essay explores the home-grown myths of the wild man and associations to wandering, linguistic confusion or plain incomprehension, and other aberrations, such as size or colour (the signifier of "dark" or "black" is important here). Burke (2004) links it to animal metaphors and ascriptions, with interesting discursive shifts from the wild man to the savage, characterised, amongst other attributes, by their "senseless words".

Grafton (1992) shows how those ancient categories and texts upon which Europeans drew when describing the then modern world, began to lose authority. The medieval world adopted the strategy of "wonder" (or marvel) as one possible response to the otherness of the other, when phenomena simply fell through the existing cultural grid. Many, unable to cope with the influx of new information from a New World, simply pulled down the mental shutters (Elliott, 1970). Grafton (1992) suggests that "the texts [i.e., ancient texts] provided European intellectuals not with a single grid that imposed a uniform order on all new information, but with a complex set of overlapping stencils, a rich and delicate set of patterns and contrivances" (p. 58). There were undoubted wars of interpretation. Humanists, for instance, contested the definitions of received "canon" in the universities and beyond and established newer, more secularised world horizons. As scepticism gained ground, monsters became less monstrous, at least in the grand sense. Amongst their achievements was to question traditional designations of other peoples (Europe's barbarians). German humanists, for example, rediscovered the historian Tacitus, because of his questioning of the traditional, Roman binary view of the German tribes as Barbarians. Tacitus reversed the picture, accusing the Romans of savagery, and so the German humanists could elevate or rehabilitate their contemporary position as a people. In the New World, there were those who saw the Spanish as being the true barbarians and who saw in the Indian a potential Christian far purer than his European counterpart. This was one aspect of the myth of the Noble Savage, which gained considerable influence in later European writings. However, a major, if not the most central, part in the questioning and erosion of classical cultural grids, was their inconsistency, as much as any new "facts" encountered. America and other "discovered places" raised new questions. In his balanced appraisal, Grafton concludes, "ancient texts provided not only the intellectual foundations of European hegemony, but also the sharpest challenges to it" (p. 354). Elliot (1970) argues that classical cosmologies lived on and that new discoveries affected Europeans slowly; the case of China and the existence of Chinese religion is an interesting one, in so far as it exercised the minds of philosophers and boosted religious scepticism. The wider intellectual consequences of human multiplicity started to be felt, even if gradually and unevenly. It should also be noted that monstrous depictions were not the sole preserve of Europeans; the Chinese, for example, had their own version of Plinian races, and the Japanese saw Europeans as "southern barbarians" and drew the Dutch as monstrously bloated figures (Burke, 2004). And then there were regional attributions, within countries. Everyone was at it.

"From darkness to promote me ...?"[7]
Frankenstein's progeny, the articulate monster

1818 saw the birth of two remarkable monsters. The first, a monster assembled from composite human parts and brought to life by electric current, Frankenstein's progeny; the other a new genre, that of the science fiction novel—a hybrid and a book that traversed the genres of romanticism and the gothic. Nothing comes out of nowhere, and the manufactured monster, also referred to as fiend, creature, daemon, whom Mary Shelley invented was a radical transformation of the stock character of the Gothic villain; it is also remarkable, given the time, that she was a twenty-one-year-old female. Shelley could not have foreseen the consequences of what she had created in literature. In our century some people mistakenly use the word "Frankenstein" to refer to the monster rather than its creator, and our imagery is indelibly influenced by the lens of twentieth-century cinematic representation. In the light of this, it is instructive to return to the novel and some of its informing context.

The later part of the eighteenth century was a high tide for Gothic novels and saw a peaking of interest in aesthetic theory. Somewhat earlier (1757), Edmund Burke (1990) published *Philosophical Enquiry into the Origins of Our Ideas of the Sublime and the Beautiful*. In it he speculates on contradictory aspects of the sublime, including delight and horror, pleasure and terror, and its capacity to arouse our "strongest emotions". Burke touches on the sense of dread, unfamiliarity, and obscurity that were to figure large in Freud's (1919) influential psychoanalytic essay on the uncanny (*unheimliche*)—that which is un-homely and sinister. Central to Burke's view is that of affective negativity, an aspect of what Botting (2014) calls "negative aesthetics". The monster gives negative shape to our fears. And we, in turn, fear its shape.

Victor Frankenstein's monster is abhorrent in conception, form, and consequence. As for form, he is the oversized product of a wretched assembly, made from the body parts of several people stitched together, and animated by electrical current. Victor recoils at the birth of a being "more hideous than belongs to humanity", lamenting the "demoniacal corpse to which I had so miserably given life" (Shelley, 2012, p. 70). And if this is the case, then Victor wonders whether he has created an entirely "new species".

Botting (2014, p. 94) observes that in terms of indirect narrative structure (different narrators, use of letters and stories), the novel is far from conventional, in fact, mirroring the monster, is "assembled from bits and pieces". Feminist writers have suggested that the novel in fact subverts the male, Romantic ideal of the author, in full control (authorship) of what they write (for a good review, see Long Hoeveler, 2004). Of course, Victor Frankenstein creates but does not control. With a predilection for science, a dubious interest in natural philosophy and alchemy, and a fascination with electricity, he confesses to many "lords of my imagination" (p. 33). Spending "days and nights in vaults and charnel-houses", the young Victor studies principles of human life and decay and resolves, against initial doubts, "to make a being of gigantic stature" (p. 47). Bringing life to this being, Victor recoils at his own act and the wretch who at first can only mutter inarticulate sounds. I will not describe the story in detail, as its outlines are familiar. However, the theme of an illegitimate creation is at the heart of a novel that plays with the consequences of Victor as "author of unalterable evils" (p. 89). The consequences bear upon fundamental questions of the era, about the worlds of nature, society, and the preservation of order. Watching and learning from his human neighbours, the monster comes (learns) to appreciate sentiment and sympathy and, in time, language. Although he remains a nameless monster, he becomes a most articulate, if naive monster; after all, he is merely trying to find a home amongst people, even if self-pity falls to revenge. Keenly aware of the reactions to him by society, he bemoans, "And what was I? Was I, then, a monster, a blot upon the earth, from which all men fled and whom all men disowned?" (p. 119), and, elsewhere, "I was benevolent and good; misery made me a fiend" (p. 152). An abused child, as it were, becomes an abusive grown up (Mellor, 2003). Not only this, but the story can be linked to the rehabilitation of the wild man image, or the noble savage who lives in a state uncorrupted by society. The demon appeals to contractual obligation (a version of social contract theory? See Cantor, 1984), as might obtain between a father to his son, or from the King to his subjects. In the twists of torment between the creator and the created, the demon explains,

"All men hate the wretched ... yet you, my creator, detest and spurn me, thy creature, to whom thou art bound by ties only dissoluble by the annihilation of one of us" (p. 97).

All manufacture requires material. And the manufacture and source material of Shelley's novel is the subject of considerable scholarship. It is usually misleading to privilege or isolate one informing context over another and this section has no desire so to do, in its brief reference to monstrous threats to social order and the images of the revolutionary mob.[8]

As ominous doubles, Botting (1991, p. 47) has observed that "monsters appear in literature and political writings to signal both a terrible threat to established rules and a call to arms that demands the confirmation and protection of authorised values". As far as we can tell, Shelley grappled with the radical ideas she was raised with and surrounded by—her parents were both associated with the radial cause, not to mention her husband Percy, with his different kind of idealism—and she was exposed to the pressing social and philosophical debates of the era. Could the novel then be symbolic, a warning about group violence, even if it is framed in a non-political, psychological manner? The use of monster imagery was certainly present in many current political representations, including of course the writings of Edmund Burke, for whom the revolution in France was characterised as the revolt of a "swinish multitude". Homegrown radicals were also seen as a monstrous threat to Britain's order and Ship of State, a view bitterly contested by the English radicals (including Mary's mother, Mary Wollstonecraft) who reversed the accusations, portraying the aristocracy instead as the true monster (Botting, 1991; Sterrenburg, 1979). Indeed, according to Sterrenburg (op. cit.) democracy itself can be seen as a monstrous threat to order that might devour those who allow it. Revolution, according to the conservatives, overthrows the legitimate, natural order (for more on revolution, see Chapter Five). Corporeal images were an integral part of political discourse, including the deformed body, as in references, again on the radical side, as it were, to "Great Beasts" of monarchy, "ulcers" of injustice, and the "monster of despotism" (de Baecque, 1993). The language of disease had been used centuries before in relation to heresy and now it had a new, political twist.

So, *Frankenstein* as political monster? Perhaps. What is true is that the novel bursts all frames, exceeding and overthrowing the normal order of things. Most of all, I would suggest, the question persists of who or what is really grotesque? Is it the hapless monster or his creator, who violates any traditional concept of creation, be it religious, procreative, and so forth? And what is grotesque? Is it the individual, be it beast or misguided creator, or is it society itself that seeks to exile a being who is both different but also alike in common humanity?

"A foul and pestilent congregation"[9]: deformity re-defined

Images of freaks have a long history, emergent from that of the monster who preceded them (Wind, 1998). Thereafter, monster is used more metaphorically, as in "human monster", the beast within, whereas the freak and oddity inherits the new actuality, even if they have always been around, so to speak. They do not need to be searched for, or found in distant lands, because they live in towns and villages, in the form of the humpback, cripple, dwarf, clubfoot, imbecile, and so on. In the seventeenth century, deformity was once more recovered by religious connotation, with Crawford (2005) tracing its connection to Protestant/Catholic divisions, such as the use of the metaphor of the "monstrous body politic" and fables of divine punishment. The "multiple bodies" of Christendom (e.g., Luther as seven-headed monster, as anti-Christ, or, on the other side of the "Papal Ass", also an anti-Christ) were, to many, an indication of the coming of "end times", and confusion and division of religions were its omen (Hsia, 2004). Along similar lines, Wind (1998) argues that part of the wider fascination of the deformed individual was that they represented a world turned upside down and out of harmony with itself; and warnings all around, where even the cleft palate might be seen as symbolic warning, such as a caution against lewd talk. In spite of this, from the scene of court entertainment, or in the depiction by certain European artists, and "scientific" attempts to classify oddities (Ambrose Paré's famous treatise describes "things outside nature"),[10] an evolution of attitudes took place. A new kind of sympathy emerged, so that in the case of the Spanish court, in the mid-seventeenth century 100 dwarfs and fools (which would have included the retarded) were listed, but by the eighteenth century there were just five. Sentiments of sympathy had been articulated much earlier, in the late sixteenth century, with essayists such as Montaigne asserting, "what we call monsters are not so to God, who sees in the immensity of His work the infinity for forms he has comprised in it" (quoted in Wind, 1998), or in Bacon's 1597 essay, *Of Deformity*, which asserts that the scornful mistreatment of the deformed leads in turn to their reactive traits, such as malice or virtue. The treatment of those who became popular sources of entertainment also became an issue, eventually, within the nineteenth-century spectacle of the freak show.

Freaks

The term freak, which previously signified whimsy or fancy, was by the 1840s, so argues Thompson (1996), equivalent to "human corporeal anomaly". We were entering the long era of the freak show and its new cast of characters: Siamese twins, bearded ladies, giants, savages, leopard-man, dog-faced boy, microcephalics, fat ladies, Aztecs, the Elephant Man, Tom Thumb, missing links, Fiji mermaid, nondescripts.

Between the 1840s and 1914, the freak show, or sideshow, gained huge popularity as a form of entertainment, in America and England in particular. With industrialisation and urbanisation, shows of such nature were no longer tethered to market places, courts, and taverns, but could travel and adapt, using even shop windows, in an earlier version perhaps of today's "pop up shop"; "Freak shows flourished, no longer dependent upon local anomalous births" (Durbach, 2010, p. 3). Such shows had appeal across social classes, sexes, and ages, and coincided, in Britain and elsewhere, with the emergence of several other spaces and places of leisure, such as the seaside town, music hall, pleasure garden, and zoo. Some ran special viewings, such as for unaccompanied ladies. In America, the freak shows began in the early 1840s, when P. T. Barnum established the American Museum. Several elements proved vital for the survival of the tradition that he initiated. Exhibits were living and were presented as "rare spectacles". Novelty and variation were essential, as interest and taste could tire, and took many forms, such as "ten-in-one" shows. Freaks might be seen engaging in an activity, such as an armless man making something. An oddly shaped couple might be presented in a domestic, bourgeois setting, making tea, and enacting a scene from everyday life. The life histories of exhibits might be advertised, and colourful props and scenery would enhance the effect, such as a primitive in the jungle or an Indian in a supposed Aztec environment. They were shown alongside other entertainers, such as contortionists and sword eaters, or together with gaffed freaks, such as a man with a hidden extra leg. Supposed professors and medics were quoted by showmen ("barkers" in circus lingo), who crafted spiels, informative and dramatic, thereby building expectation and delivering shock. In an instance of how technology assisted change in the leisure industry, the development of "set-plate" techniques in photography enabled mass production of prints from one exposure. Human oddities were reproduced in photographs and leaflets, and the collecting of *"carte de visites"* ("visiting cards") became hugely popular. The era of the "album" had arrived, often featuring visiting cards if this nature. A number of social historians (e.g., Bogdan, 1988; Cook, 1996) have carefully elucidated the many and ingenious ways in which the show and the exhibit were constructed in practice. One should not simplify the wide possible functions of such spectacles, but here two aspects are noted.

One concerns the role of expectation and gaze. Barnum, and the others, excelled at developing an art of presentation, of staging and build-up, of exoticising, and hence evoking a sense of mystery about what the audiences were about to behold. The range was vast, including racialised freaks, primitives, and "missing links". Julia Pastrada (advertised variously as "Hybrid Indian!" "The misnomered Bear Woman", "Monkey women", "nondescript") a Mexican woman with severe deformity and covered with hair, became an international sensation, her mummified remains being a source of public curiosity until her final homecoming for burial 150 years after her death. The link to ugliness and repellent femininity figured in the mix (the "world's ugliest women" was not a rare slogan). The black American, Henry Johnson was also a "nondescript"; "in both its name ('What is It?') and its ingeniously evasive classification-type ('nondescript'), Barnum's early 1860 hybrid both literally and figuratively begged the pubic to fill in the blanks" (Cook, 1996, p. 140).[11] Given the context of the era in America, the language is chilling. Yet, the process of the gaze represented, instantiated, a source of social power and positioning. In Victorian culture, there was a growing interest, for example, in the notion of the "average man", itself a statistical creation of the Belgian mathematician and sociologist, Adolphe Quetelet. Beyond the confines of science, consider the related circulation of notions of the "norm(al)", the "type", the "manly", the "able bodied", and their alternatives within the culture (Craton, 2009). Galton's eugenics and theories of degeneration were also influenced by this cultural plexus. Fahy's (2006, p. 22) careful examination of the culture and literature of freaks makes the point that "freak shows used various methods to establish a clear, comfortable distance between audience and spectacle".

All shows come to an end and the freak show was no exception. Given its course in Britain, from the late 1840s to the eve of World War One, it was a long run. But by its tail-end, tastes had changed, attitudes and sensitivity had shifted, and the leisure industry transformed. Freaks moved from the realm of public spectacle to that pathology, from the fairs to the laboratory and the medical theatre. Freaks had been demythologised, objectified, rendered safe for secular inquiry. For example, Joseph Merrick, the famous Elephant Man, was shown, nakedly, as a case to the London Pathological Society in 1884.[12] Sentiments had changed, and his earlier capture by a Belgian circus entertainer considered an outrage against an innocent, or so the story goes. In the realm of entertainment, shows at Earls Court exhibition arenas featuring freaks were stopped in 1907 (although at Olympia, another exhibition centre nearby, the practice continued until the 1920s). As to its decline, there are many reasons why, including the impact of war and its devastating, visible injures, the rise of disability rights, but also new sources of entertainment, such as the cinema, which effectively absorbed the monsters (Fahy, 2006). On the silver screen, a new generation of imagined monsters stepped forward. *Frankenstein* reappeared in the 1931 Universal Pictures movie, although the cranking monster made famous by Boris Karloff, as well as the story, were a far cry from Shelley's novel; *Dracula* appeared in 1931, loosely based on Bram Stoker's novel. Freaks were excised from the vocabulary, though were readmitted in new forms in the comics and hippie culture of the 1960s. "Freaking out" became an experience, and "freaks" an assorted medley of unkempt, long-haired characters who challenged authority and the world of "straights".

Conclusion

The nature and place of monsters changes over time and between cultures. We have touched on a few only, including the spectacular beings of the Middles Ages and beyond, the monsterisation of certain human groups, the literary aesthetics of the grotesque, and the spectacle of the deformed. The deformed and the freaks, like the monsters before them, were still reminders of sorts, likely serving a reassuring function for their spectators; "The monster is a concept that we need in order to tell ourselves what we are *not*" (Hanifi, 2000, p. 218). We and they fall either side of the narrative partitions that we invent.

There are still plenty of monsters, but their passage into toys, characters in games, and figures within film and science fiction, is another story. They are thoroughly tamed—"As soon as one perceives a monster in a monster, one begins to domesticate it" (Derrida, 1995, p. 386). I have sought to show something of the narrative aspects of monsters and the fascination they evoke. It is a complicated story of distorted mirroring and separations, distinctions, emotions, fears, and reassurances, even if the nature of what is so represented always changes.

Notes

1. In a fascinating paper, Ballesteros Gonzalez (1996) suggests that Shelley's *Frankenstein* was inspired by the imagery of *Richard III*. Ironically, with the discovery of Richard III's actual body by archaeologists, doubt has been cast on the actual extent and visibility of his deformity.
2. Historian Herlihy (1997), points out that the Black Death, itself not a word used in the Middle Ages but rather by later chroniclers, was an unprecedented human disaster, reducing the population in many areas by half and even more. As for the social fissures it created, he points out that the plague "caused divisions between the healthy and the sick; between those in the cultural mainstream and its margins, namely, strangers, travellers, beggars, lepers and Jews; between the mass of society and its cultural leaders, its governors, priests, and physicians" (p. 59). It changed attitudes towards death, no longer the "kind caretaker" but more readily the ravishing monster. In an important point about the role of borders, in periods of plague cities often closed their gates to travellers and expelled beggars, prostitutes, and other undesirables. Help, healing, and atonement, sometimes dramatic, as with the flagellants, became major concerns or activities.
3. The quotation is from Chaucer's (2005) *The Prioress's Tale* which uses common anti-Jewish rhetoric and tropes, such as the charge of "shameful profit" (usury) and influence by the "serpent Satan". In repeating and referencing a child murder, a male perpetrator, and a boy victim, the story sets up the dichotomy of Christian innocence/vulnerability against Jewish treachery/malevolence. The setting of the tale in the East, somewhere Asiatic, also suggests an anti-Islamic motif, in a doubling up of malign referents (Delany, 2002). Indeed, as for the latter, Muslims were sometimes represented as cynocephali, a dog-headed race, as in "heathen hounds". As for anti-Semitic motifs, Langmuir (1990) provides a useful analysis of Chaucer's tale, whilst Nirenberg

(2013) impressively excavates the wider formation of anti-Jewish tropes in history.

4. Terms such as "grotesque", "ugly" are post-medieval, and it is difficult to find equivalent terms for the actual period. "Ugly" derives from the Norse *uggling*, something to be feared, and "grotesque" a derivation from grotto (Bovey, 2002). Ugliness is of course a trope that applied to (most) monsters, including witches and the Devil himself; "Beauty follows rules, ugliness breaches them" (Eco, 2007, p. 94). The beautification and taming of monsters is, however, another side to this, as in the twentieth century creation of the "cuddly monster" and child's toy, which have proliferated. On a recent trip to the supermarket I spotted three (children's) DVDs on one stand—*Monsters Inc, Monster University,* and *Monsters v Aliens*.

5. The Biblical figure of Cain, famed in Hebrew and Christian traditions, was punished, "marked" by deformity by God, sometimes in the form of horns, at other times lumps. Although excluded from the world, at one level, his real power is that he continued to haunt it (Cohen, 2012). This is a fascinating story, mixed as it was with other legends, for all kinds of reasons, not least in its dreadful implications for the history of disability. Of note, in Gregory IX's Papal decree of 1234, "high order" was denied to candidates showing disfigurement or blemishes.

6. The quotation is from Christopher Columbus' journal entry for Friday 12 October 1492 (Markham, 2010, pp. 36–37).

7. The quotation is from Milton's *Paradise Lost* ("Did I request thee, maker, from my clay/To mould me man, did I solicit thee / From darkness to promote me ...?" (Milton, 2004, Book X, lines 734–735).

8. In a valuable, if speculative paper on *Frankenstein,* Malchow (1993) examines the demonisation of the proletariat and fears of Luddite revolts in early eighteenth-century England. One could link this in terms of a theory of an "exclusionary matrix" (Weegmann, 2014) to Jacobins and widespread fears unleashed by the revolutions in France. Malchow adds a further aspect of interest, that of prevalent images of the Negro body and anxiety surrounding slavery and its potential abolition. He traces the staging of *Frankenstein* in Victorian theatre, as well as in print, and with it the perpetuation of the racialised Other as monster or brute.

9. The quotation is from Shakespeare's *Hamlet* (2:ii).

10. Ambrose Paré was chief surgeon to Charles IX of France, whose *On Monsters and Marvels* (1634) is a "scientific", or at least systematic document, detailing an infinite variety of natural wonder, with captions such as " half-man, half-swine", "a very monstrous animal known in Africa", "counterfeiting hedge-whores", "demons who live in quarries

or mines", "two-headed child", "flying monsters" and "celestial monsters". Paré also scrutinised the available body and reproductive mishaps, but his work represents a cultural break. Treatises on monsters and teratology became a genre and, as Wittkower (1942, p. 66) points out, Paré and his contemporaries, were "focused on the Aristotelian conception that nothing can happen ... at random".

11. Johnson, who had learning disability and microcephaly, was paraded with a fur suit, shaven head, stick, and pseudo-exotic backdrop. The exhibition lasted eight years, with Johnson a long-term employee. In the spiels and photographic cards about him, he was said to have been captured from Africa, where he had been living in a tree.

12. Joseph Merrick's life is a good example of the production of the "freak" at a cultural crossroads, although our image of him, like others, is unavoidably influenced by film (1980, by David Lynch). In her careful examination of contemporary accounts of Merrick, including his autobiographical notes, Crockford (2010, p. 43), traces the ambiguities of freak/human, the efforts to define him "as either and both deformed object and martyred subject". The public gaze to which he was exposed is part of the fascination: the man who attracts the interest of aristocrats and royalty; the amusement and revulsion of the public; letters to *The Times*; shock but also dedicated kindness of nursing staff (he was granted living quarters at the London Hospital, nowadays the Royal London, Whitechapel); and the continual stream of medical observers, from those of learned societies to medical students. Before his fame, he was exhibited in a shop in Whitechapel, reluctantly at first, as the renowned promoter, Tom Norman (English counterpart to Barnum), thought him too shocking to display. An accompanying leaflet explained that his deformity resulted from his mother being startled by an elephant during pregnancy. One dimension not explored by Crockford, however, is the possible role of contemporary identification and guilt surrounding the many exploited and abject figures of nineteenth-century society (the poor, the industrial multitude, the immigrant, street children, and so on). The issue of freak exploitation is also debated by some, who point to the fame and relative economic success of a small minority of freaks. It is, after all, tempting to paint the Victorian period itself as monstrous for its ill treatment of many.

CHAPTER FOUR

"Naught but a story to tell"*: Alcoholics Anonymous

Alcoholics Anonymous (hereafter, AA) is a worldwide fellowship for those seeking recovery from alcoholism. It is a unique and enduring form of mutual help, with its democratic structures, self-governing ethos, and independence from the professional and institutional worlds. AA meetings, and their related practices, provide stable and consistent conditions within which members can overcome the dysregulation, damage, and poor self-care that lie at the heart of addictive suffering. AA meetings are centred on the telling and transmission of salient experiences and stories. Stories allow coherence to grow and meaning to be made of past troubles and current hope. Through immersion in a process of change, viable narratives of recovery are built.

"AA is a fellowship of men and women who share their experience, strength and hope with each other that they may solve their common

---

*In an early address to the medical community, Bill W., the co-founder of AA, said that "… the 400 pages of *Alcoholics Anonymous* contain no theory. … Being laymen, we have naught but a story to tell" (Bill W, 1944).

problem and help others to recover from alcoholism." So reads part of the preamble that is quoted at the start of all meetings of AA.

When MacIntyre (1984) said that human beings "are story telling animals", he expressed an assumption at the heart of narrative theory, as did Oscar Wilde, who drew attention to the aesthetic "shaping" of experience, that "life imitates art". To narrate (from the Latin *narrare*, "to recount" and "to know"), means that events and experiences are structured in time sequences and organised coherently. In overcoming addictions—indeed, many other disorders—people need convincing "narratives of recovery" that help them see themselves in a new way and provide a meaningful account of their struggles and achievements. Like having a map, narratives help with navigation but do not guarantee a problem-free journey. As White (White, Laudet & Becker, 2006, p. 18) puts it: "In the transition from addiction to recovery, each client must find ways to draw life meaning and purpose ... [to] forge new prescriptions for daily living, and generate hope for the future."

I specialised in substance misuse for twenty years and have a long association with AA, in recent years as trustee and professional friend. My analysis reflects this location, as a psychologist, not himself in recovery, as a psychotherapist, and as a specialist in the field.

AA history: "on the anvils of group experience"[1]

Like any good idea, the origins of AA are ordinary. AA effectively began in mid-1930s Akron, Ohio, when two struggling drinkers—a medic ("Dr. Bob") and stock-broker ("Bill W.")—turned to each other, sharing accounts of their struggles with alcohol. Something transformational happened in so far as from these efforts at self-honesty and testimony, they, and soon others, were enabled to rebuild shattered lives. The embryo of what was to become AA, with one alcoholic helping another, was present in these simple acts of meeting, sharing, and acceptance. Stigma and marginalisation of alcoholics was widespread, and arguably, post-prohibition, America was ripe for a "new paradigm" of care (Levine, 1978). Fitting then, that it was a mutual-help fellowship that grew in spite of, or perhaps because of, the inhospitable soil.

There were many social, cultural, and philosophical influences on AA, in a curious mix of incident, chance, and charisma (Kurtz, 1982). AA forged discourses of sickness, replacing those of sinfulness, so that alcoholism could be rescued from moral condemnation and historical associations with degeneration, weak will, and so on; its "trouble" could be thought about in new ways. A wider narrative emerged, that of alcoholism as a progressive illness and a programme of personal recovery for those who wanted it badly enough.

AA is a lay tradition of psychosocial support. Although AA has no creed on the "true nature" of alcoholism, and its members do not sign up to any particular "theory" of it, the alcoholic is generally seen as suffering from a form of malady of body, mind, and soul, a malady with a progressive course. AA blends biomedical, psychosocial, and spiritual ideas together (Miller & Kurtz, 1994). It is a form of pragmatism, in so far as AA enables problem drinkers to change "a day at a time" and, in so doing, to revise the story of themselves, as "alcoholics in recovery". Once drinkers stop drinking, and embark on a journey of change, they can transcend previous disorder, lack of self-regulation and its associated postures of blame, denial, self-sufficiency, etc. It takes courage to face the consequences of past behaviour and to conceive of a different kind of future, with putting down the bottle being just the beginning. AA invites rigorous examination of behaviour and self, addressing entrenched lifestyles and well-practised defences of disavowal, defiance, and so on. The idea of facing a serious, cumulative crisis, or "hitting bottom", is emphasised as a condition of change. In psychodynamic terms, one could translate the emphasis on admitting "powerlessness" in Step One as a breaking down of omnipotence, or in the words of the first psychiatric friend of AA, Henry Tiebout (1944), a process of "ego reduction". With regard to the significance of such personal crises, Bill W. was influenced by reading William James, and other psychologists of the era. The cultivation of humility is central in AA, as a process of self-acceptance and "humanising" oneself.

There is a spiritual, as distinct from religious, dimension to AA recovery. Changing one's patterns means changing one's attitudes and acknowledging the serious imbalances created by drinking, expressed metaphorically as the "dis-ease" of alcoholism. Carl Jung, who briefly corresponded with Bill W. (1967), had also encapsulated an idea of alcoholism as (amongst others things) "sickness of the soul", when he pointed out *spiritus contra spiritum* ("spirits drive out spirituality"). Recovery demands a personal revolution of sorts, including facing difficult truths and consequences, and reparation ("making amends") where this is possible or wise, and connection too, letting others in, in new ways. Without this deeper level of change, evasion occurs and real progress is blocked; the distinction in AA between being "dry" and being "sober" (the latter with its attendant "peace of mind"), reflects this.

AA invites a way of living one's life rather than being a "treatment" and is thus more than "relapse prevention". There are many dimensions to change in AA, and each member fashions his or her recovery. Not that change is always easy to make sense of; in the words of a colleague in (long-term) recovery, "I know the reality of recovery in AA, though I don't understand it". Progress is intimately concerned with care of self, through connection with others in similar situations, and the Twelve Steps of AA are like scaffolds that invite such change, away from the "user" of the past and towards a more secure future. In this way, AA fosters new knowledge of "oneself as another" (to borrow a phrase from philosopher Paul Ricoeur, 1992), premised on attention to mutual vulnerabilities and strengths (so-called "character defects and assets"). From anecdotal observations of many (open) AA meetings, I see a mixture of reassuring, impersonal fellowship (structures, democratic traditions, practices that transcend the individual, as in the Greek *koinonia*—communion, to "have a share in something") and a deeply personal programme of recovery. In the words of one participant in a study of long-term change, "AA is like a loose-fitting garment ... I find myself, somehow, within it, find what is useful for me ..." (Weegmann & Piwowoz-Hjort, 2009a, p. 291).

What are, then, some of the ingredients of change?

AA: group therapy

All groups, with any client group, from the psycho-educational to the analytic, from the structured and time-limited to the unstructured and "slow-open", have their own norms of interaction, leadership—or its absence—and what can be called "speech-acts", that is, discursive norms (forms of speech, if one wills) as to what constitutes a contribution and act of sharing. We have previously looked at speech-act theory in the first chapter. In AA meetings there are rather particular discursive norms and structures (O'Halloran, 2008), beginning with a reading of the AA preamble (see the excerpt at the start of the chapter), with its emphasis on commonality and the sharing of "experience, strength and hope", and ending with the Serenity Saying, where people are encouraged to balance acceptance and change. Following a "main share" by a nominated speaker (agreed in advance), for up to fifteen minutes, the meeting is opened up by the chair (all posts rotate in AA) for others to share their own "experience, strength and hope", as indicated by hand-raising. Sharing in AA is an invitation for identification with the main share and revelation of one' struggles, achievements, week' progress, events and so forth. There is no debate or "cross-talk", with each person addressing just their situation. There are numerous other conventions and variations, depending on the nature of the meeting, such as an invitation to "shy sharers" to talk if they wish, specific Step meetings, readings from AA literature, and the Twelve Steps and Twelve Traditions (often other AA sayings as well) are displayed on wall posters.

At first sight, this is quite different from the professional therapy group. But, of course, there are group therapeutic factors in all groups, such as identification, modelling, inspiration, instillation of hope, and others. Indeed, the content of groups may be secondary to the process. In the group analytic language with which I am familiar, there is a process of resonance, exchange, and reciprocity, richly expressed in AA's emphasis to "look for similarities not differences" and in the encouragement of identification. Then again, the interpersonal group tradition has been more influential in conceptualising our understanding of how therapeutic bonding and learning together occurs, including in AA (Flores, 1988). The particular speech act surrounding the address— "Hello, my name is … and I'm alcoholic", is an example of ritualised group identification and a reminder. One could also think about such identifications in terms of a process of "twin-ship", relating to what one has in common with one's "fellows" (Flores, op. cit.). From observation of open meetings, I notice an ordered rhythm that, in following a set practice, allows the individual to find a unique voice, an example of a predictable (i.e., structure) unpredictable (i.e., the shares) generative process. In other words, whilst the structure remains the same, each meeting is different. There is a process of "self-soothing" in this innovative familiarity, tapping into human needs for affiliation and acceptance (Robinson, 1996). There are many other aspects to group process in AA meetings and it is important to acknowledge the wider milieu in which meetings take place, including their regularity, association with other meetings, the "pre-meeting" welcome, "post-meeting" socialisation, coffees, and so on. The discursive exchanges between members, in formal and non-formal time, help create a sense of solidarity that, when internalised, can sustain individuals through the many challenges they face. Learning toleration of self (inner toleration, toleration of affect, etc.) and others (listening, connecting with, learning) is a vital constituent of developing the art of "sober dialogue" (Weegmann & English, 2010). And it is sober dialogue that enables the building of new narratives of recovery.

AA: psychosocial change

Although distinct in its culture and governed by a host of lay tradition and practice, change in AA involves some similar processes of change as those addressed by professional therapies, including behavioural change, cognitive reconstruction, building alternatives to the drinking lifestyle, self-efficacy, and so forth.

There are many sayings in fellowship oral and written tradition, sayings which offer footholds and reminders to those forging a path away from addiction. They form what could, in the language of Russian (Vygotskian) psychology, be termed "scaffolding" (McLeod, 2010), suggestions that support developmental change and identify risk. Consider some instances. "Recovery is a journey ... not a destination" is a reminder of recovery as an ongoing process rather than an event, encouraging continuing work on the self whilst avoiding complacency. The Narcotics Anonymous saying, "Time to change your playmates, playgrounds, and playthings" succinctly challenges the ingrained habits of using and its lifestyles, as does the equivalent in AA, "To avoid slipping, avoid slippery people, slippery places, and slippery things." Such therapeutic reminders can be thought of as attempts to guide memories, and aid relapse prevention. Swora's (2001) paper suggests that just as alcoholism damages memory and social relations, the AA programme, including sayings, creates a positive and alternative "community of memory". Finally, consider the saying, "I have found that the process of discovering who I really am begins with knowing who I really don't want to be." This is an evocative message, pointing to the importance of forging a "non-using" identity and consolidating the transition and disidentification (as distinct from denial) from the active drinker and person of the past associated with it. This is not to simplify the AA programme of change, which consists of more than attending meetings and the use of sayings, although, as is argued, the latter help the person to recognise common dilemmas and learn from a wider cultural capital. Those who do commit and actively involve themselves in recovery can find a real sense of community and belonging from AA fellowship.

AA: structure of care and regulation

As is noted, there are formal and informal aspects of care in AA, from greetings to meetings, personal programmes of recovery, networks, sponsors, service, and, of course, friendship. We have touched upon how acceptance of mutual vulnerabilities, strengths, and talents help individuals to overcome the isolation and deep wounds to which addiction has led. This is part and parcel of what can be called a wider "structure of care" in AA.

If addiction is a disorder of self-regulation (Khantzian & Mack, 1989), recovery requires, by definition, new ways of caring for and regulating the self. And just as addiction characteristically isolates individuals, recovery invites reconnection and reintegration within new or previously damaged relationships—a journey from omnipotence (or impotence) to mutuality. Mack (1981) develops a useful notion of "self-governance", which he defines as a group of functions concerned with choosing, evaluating, planning, and responsibility, broadly speaking, and how problems in these areas ("unmanageability") are addressed by AA. Rightly, he underlines that "self-regulation" (for all of us) is dependent on the presence of helpful *others*, of what he calls a "self-other context". Those in recovery grow in confidence as they re-take ownership and management of their lives. The sharing practices and social structures of AA fellowship provide for graded experiences and responsibilities which run counter to previous substance-using lifestyles and degraded forms of relationship.

AA as narrative change

Clients with substance issue problems experience serious "biographical disruption" (Bury, 1982) of their lives, to put it mildly. And as their problems accrue, there are more difficulties with which to contend; half a lifetime, easily, of silted-up consequences. Erikson's (1963) classic "life-stages" approach concerns the growing, formation, maintenance, and passing on of viable and accomplished identity; with alcoholism one may not be able to characterise one's life in healthy and productive ways, with past achievements being over-shadowed by the drinking present. Good early experiences promote, in Erikson's view, an enduring legacy of hope, a kind of narrative optimism, if one wills. When drug or alcohol dependence set in however, normal sources of identity are unpicked and horizons of experience are reduced. As a person is caught in a cycle of decline, hope in an alternative recedes. Ultimately, the person is left with all the dilemmas of what sociologists call "spoiled identity" (Goffman, 1963). One drinker, looking back over his life, commented, "I'm getting nowhere, very fast. Everything I had is gone and anything I had is wasted. What have I got to show for the last twenty years?"

When the stranglehold of the drug is broken and the person begins to change, narrative adjustment helps in the figuring out of a way forward and the construction of a meaningful life. In AA, this is sometimes called "a pathway to normal living". In other words, those who exit addictive careers construct ways of accounting for their former activities and "condition" in order to be able to move on. Former lives are re-evaluated and so too are "former selves" (i.e., a story of "how I was then" versus "how I am now"). Biernacki (1986) refers to the "identity work" that is involved in resolving drug addiction, and others have looked at the construction of a "non-addict" identity in detail, whereby previous behaviour and current lifestyle are re-evaluated (McIntosh & McKeganey, 2000). The "shadow" of a chronic disorder is long one and recovery requires a remarkable readaptation and revision of personal identity. With growing recovery time and increased confidence, however, people are able to articulate more elaborate narratives, supported by collective stores of narrative, such as those provided by AA fellowship groups. In other words, personal stories of recovery are not solely created in the minds of individuals, but resonate with, and draw from, wider cultural resources. AA provides "narrative capital", practical wisdom and forms of coherence/consistency that are not easily found elsewhere, which help reverse the inconsistency and incoherence of the past. Narrative identity, in the way in which I mean it here, relates to, "an individual's internalised, evolving, and integrative story of the self" (McAdams, 2008).

The AA saying previously quoted ("I have found that the process of discovering who I really am begins with knowing who I really don't want to be") concerns a dialectic between the "who I am" from the "who I really don't want to be", illustrating the key role of narrative identity. Harré (1997, p. 177) argues that it is through narratives that are expressed the "sort of person one is, what one's strengths and weaknesses are and what one's life has been", and, moreover, given that the self-concept is linked to the "stories we tell about ourselves", the actions one performs as oneself. As a mutual help fellowship, AA explicitly values the importance of story (as communicated in acts of telling, sharing, and hearing). Acts of telling and hearing are not singular events, but require retelling, revision, and remembering. All this is achieved, however, not on the basis of a theory, but on a valuation of ordinary, lived experience and its telling. AA offers the canvas through which a particular voice is found; Humphreys (2000, p. 504) underlines the point that in AA, "community narratives and personal stories interact". Others refer to the use of shared conventions and a "publication", or social owning, of one's situation and efforts to change (Koski-Jännes, 2002).

These transformations in narrative identity—how people speak and figure themselves, become more unified and are critical to the recovery of a more coherent, ordered sense of auto-biography (Hänninen & Koski-Jännes, 2004). A viable "moral identity" is be forged out of the years of chaos, which is both an autobiographical achievement and a social trajectory (Harré, 2010). This is consonant with our (Weegmann & Piwowoz-Hjort, 2009 a) study of long-term recovery, in which participants progressively articulated their journeys from active substance users to "alcoholics in recovery" and how AA had, over the years, enabled such personal transformation and reconnection. Connecting the sense of narrative with the healing potential of group, Khantzian (1995, p. 164) observes, "storytelling, sharing and bearing witness to each other's distress, and the traditions of openness and honesty act as sources of comfort and support for people who otherwise would go on in their lives with their distress unnoticed, unspoken and unacknowledged".

Conclusion

Alcoholism is an imploding, disorganising, and self-undermining disorder that exposes the sufferer to serious adverse experiences, some reversible, others not. It strips personal assets and health. The concept of "post-traumatic growth" can be readily adapted to characterise the nature of abstinence and recovery from substance misuse. AA has found a way of harnessing natural group processes and identification with a shared goal in such a way that individual alcoholics can viably restructure their lives. AA enables cognitive, behavioural, and emotional change, providing a framework, a narrative structure to recovery. Without wishing to romanticise the path of recovery, "the story" can indeed be a part of what can help to set one free.

Note

1. Bill, W. (1967) uses the image of AA and its traditions as having been hammered on the "anvils of group experience". I have offered a group-analytic appreciation of AA and the Twelve Steps and Twelve Traditions elsewhere (Weegmann, 2004).

CHAPTER FIVE

Revolutionary subjects, bodies, and crowds

This chapter examines the subject and imagery of social and political revolution. By definition, a revolution, of any kind, involves at the very least a displacement of an older way, which is discarded as outmoded or reactionary, and may involve a violent overthrow and rebellion against it—a social rupture. The "revolutionary cause" is regarded by its adherents as absolutely necessary, unavoidable, and timely, in contradiction to the justifications of those defending the old order, although, in turn, revolutionary change creates new sources of discord and counter-reaction. Revolutions—both sought and feared—tell us a lot about efforts by human groups to redefine the world, and to mobilise narratives for their defence or defeat. Not only this, but the origins of "crowd psychology" are intimately mixed up with a fear of revolutionary elements in society.

"It was the best of times, it was the worst of times ..." So begins *A Tale of Two Cities*, the historical novel by Charles Dickens (1859). The cities, London and Paris, are depicted during the turmoil of the French Revolution, the revolution that represents both light and darkness, a "spring of hope" to the oppressed and a "winter of despair" to those of the *ancien régime* ("old order"). The polarity that Dickens captures so well is a theme bound up with revolution, the crowds associated with it and the potential "monsters" it displaces and unleashes. Prompted by Harold Behr's (2015) imaginative study of the French revolution, this essay goes alongside his offering, to situate the subject of revolution/revolutionary subject(s) in a wider context of history and group theory.

Revolution

The events: riot, revolt, uprising, resistance, anarchy, civil war, insurrection, revolution. The places: streets, squares, jungles, hills, barricades. The agents: masses, mobs, partisans, the people, patriots, citizens, agitators, revolutionaries. And the reversals; restoration, reaction, coups, counter-revolutions. I begin with the language of revolution and its scene of action because of the clues it contains. There is a rhetoric of revolution, from the exhilaration it inspires to the fear it engenders, points with which Dickens dramatically starts his novel, an aesthetics of upturning and overthrow (Caygill, 2013; Sharpe & Zwicker, 1998). All revolutionary movements express the imagination, with imagery of sweeping away and rebuilding, from scratch. Think of the positive side, the sense of a "justified cause", of the solidarity and dreams that revolution engenders. There is a romance that readily attaches to revolution, which may be seen as a realisation, an inexorable movement of history; consider Marx's 1848 (itself in a decade of revolutions) dramatic line that "[a] spectre is haunting Europe—the spectre of communism". In earlier versions of revolution, if that word can be used, Hobsbawm (1969) explores the mythology of social banditry and associated primitive rebels. Social banditry is in essence a form of minority rebellion in peasant societies, of outlaws who become heroes, champions, fighters for justice, and so forth. In the English context the most famous of these figures is Robin Hood, the noble robber (Dodds, 2011). Robin Hood is a malleable myth, first present from the late fourteenth century, celebrated in rhyme and ballad and vastly different to its later additions and cast of colourful characters, made even more apparent in its appropriation by twentieth century film. Hood is a liminal, underworld figure, who stands against arbitrary local authority—although, importantly, not against the King—and is linked to an Anglo-Saxon identity, an avenger of injustice. There are many such figures throughout history, Ned Kelly being a modern version, mythologised as an anti-British, political revolutionary (his father was transported from Ireland to Australia for petty theft). In some ways, the guerrillas and rural fighters replaced the outlaws. The romance of the primitive rebel is wrapped up with their language, or argot, clothing, and followers—their capes, liberty caps, rakish costumes, bravado, preferred weapons, flags, bands, and sympathisers. In part this is the story of the creation of heroes and martyrs, whose actions stretch back to antecedent movements; Jan Palach, the young student who set himself alight in the aftermath of the Prague Spring in 1968, has been linked in a symbolic chain with Jan Huss, the heretic burned at the stake in the fifteenth century, both seen as defenders of freedom and truth against despotism.

Revolutions are stylish affairs, with uniforms, codes, flags, proclamations, statues (raised and felled), badges, lifestyles, art, and languages. Symbolism is always present, as in the way in which the French Revolution created an early version of the Left and Right division and in its language of demand—"Liberté, égalité, fraternité", or, in the case of Russia, "Peace, bread, land" and "All power to the Soviets". Revolutions of the word, such as *patrie* ("homeland"), or *citoyen* ("citizen"), and "nation", are endowed with a mystical, magical quality (Burke, 2004). Then there is a literature and poetry of revolution, including of a base, scurrilous nature, such as the pornographic and the comic "pamphlet wars" that occurred on both sides during the French upheavals, just as it had in the English situation 150 years earlier. The young Wordsworth, living for a while in revolutionary France, is influenced both by personal love and by passion for the Girondist faction—who were later wiped out—and refers plaintively to "the attraction of a country in romance!" Meanwhile the radical pioneer Mary Wollstonecraft forged a powerful defence of republican virtues and argument against patriarchy in all its guises. Deploying, whilst changing, the "Rights of Man" language of Tom Paine, she addresses injustice against women and its legitimisation, the "tyranny of men" as she called it (Wollstonecraft, 2004; first published 1792). A revolutionary, "rights bearing" subjectivity was born, dubbed "Jacobin" by its detractors, but which for Wollstonecraft raised all those vital questions of the day, "the question of environment over inheritance ... female rationality ... and individual merit marked by sensibility and rationality rather than birthright" (Wallace, 2009, p. 17).

Far after the events themselves, once the market gets hold, another form of (de-political) style arises, of revolutionary nostalgia that inspires fashion brands, tee-shirts, and fills theatres (consider the ubiquitous and eternally youthful Che Guevara image or the popularity of *Les*

Misérables). Revolutions do something to time, heralding sharp breaks and instituting, at least in theory, a new order. With complete revolutions, time itself is recast, as in the abolition of so-called papist, pagan, or profane festivals (such as Christmas) during the Long Parliament in England, the invention of a revolutionary calendar in France, or, and with particularly chilling implications, Pol Pot's setting of Cambodia's clock to "year zero". With revolutionary actions and reversals, terror may come to reign, depicted in colour, such as red or white. And then there are the peaceful revolutions that occasion admiration, themselves decorated with colour and imagery—Orange revolutions, Velvet and Jasmine ones, the carnation, individuals set against tanks, the promise in words such as "Spring". Some seem cosy, such as cultural revolutions, which, depending on context, might turn out to be anything but— think only of the Maoist movement and its widespread devastations. The "imagined pure" often merges with actual purges. So there is the romance of revolutionary simplification, with its denial of a negative side—the fear, panic, disenchantment, and reversals that might follow on the heels of revolution. But critics of revolution can equally simplify the picture by defending a natural, "old order", whose own violent legacy is minimised and overlooked. After all, the French Revolution challenged the legacy of the absolutist state, which had itself consolidated in the aftermath of the devastating French wars of religion and other disorders, including peasant unrest and the *Fronde* (Anderson, 1974). As for violence, the guillotine might symbolise French revolutionary excess but was invented earlier, indeed was a mechanical replacement for the sword and the axe. Germans states had used a version of the falling axe from the seventeenth century and decapitation (capital, as in capital offence, from the Latin *capus*, head) itself is an ancient form of punishment.

An English revolution

Revolution has not always meant revolution in the sense that we know it, its contemporary meaning starting with the Glorious Revolution of 1688 (the displacement of James II and accession of William and Mary). Hill (1990) traces the term to its older, astronomic connotations, of "revolution in the heavens" or any circular movement and orbits. Nowadays, revolution is a widely used metaphor and is applied to almost any phenomena, from industrial and sexual revolutions, cognitive revolutions, art and personal revolutions, print and digital revolutions, through to the promotion of countless "revolutionary" new products on the market. Some mental health survivor networks in the 1980s even called for a "mad revolution". Going back to major upheavals however, England witnessed its own version of revolution a long time before France, even though the word was not yet used by contemporaries; instead, there was colourful talk of civil "distractions", "turmoils", "tumblings", "convulsions", and, in the terminology of the royalists, the Great Rebellion, a phrase with deliberate Biblical connotations (Rachum, 1995). Some conservatives, such as Thomas Hobbes, saw true revolution in the *restoration* of the monarchy, as only this event was a completion of a series of previous, destructive turmoil and upheavals.

The mid-seventeenth century in England witnessed some of the most remarkable developments in our history, involving the execution of King and Archbishop in the name of the people of England. This lead to the period of the commonwealth, or interregnum, and an unprecedented mushrooming of ideas, groups, and sects, each trying to articulate the moment by constructing a vision of the life that was and the soon-expected future. The abolition of censorship, for a period, enabled radical and divergent opinion to be circulated as had never occurred before. Amongst these groups, each locked into wars of interpretation, were: Diggers and Levellers, Quakers, Ranters, Fifth Monarchists, Anabaptists, and Familists. These movements have to be set against the wider context of earlier struggles to settle societal and religious life in the wake of the English reformation, in particular two visions of the "confessional state" and how men and women should relate to a national church and scripture, on one side Anglican-Royalists and on the other Puritan Parliamentarians (Morrill, 1991). This divide was itself the outcome of an earlier one, set in motion by Henry's reforms and the complex compromise that made up the Elizabethan settlement in the sixteenth century. In the time of revolution, the victorious Parliamentarians had to contend with the continued and unanticipated strength of traditional Anglicanism, divisions and competitions within Puritan and Calvinist thought, and the spread of "heretical" and separatist views. "Puritans", who sought further purification of what they regarded as the "halfly-reformed church", were a diverse group, some moderate, others radical, some remaining within the Anglican Church whilst others departed from it (Weegmann, 2014b). Amongst the countless radical views were: a questioning of the Bible (some groups publicly burned the Bible as it did not represent the Word of God; other sects allegorised the Bible to the degree that its literality was displaced, whilst for others it was *the* revolutionaries' handbook); questioning property, the traditional basis of marriage; refusing to remove hats before superiors; the raising up of the poor; and even, for a few, the challenging of male superiority. This revolutionary ferment, like many other revolutions, contained important "millennial" dimensions, such as the idea of a final lifting of the oppressive "Norman Yoke", a return to an "earlier" period or an "outside" of time (e.g., the free Anglo-Saxons, the time of the primitive and uncorrupted church)—in a real sense the completion of history. This fitted with the elimination of the mythology of the "divine right" of Kings and with the new mythology of the coming of Christ's kingdom; in the words of the radical Milton, Christ as the "shortly expected king", sweeping away "all earthly tyrannies" (Hill, 1972). Hill (1990) notes that the term "absolute" slowly changed from meaning something "perfect" or "complete" to a connotation of "unlimited power" and the "arbitrary", and hence something to be overthrown. In the memorable words of the Leveller leader, Gerrard Winstanley, these times witnessed paralleled change, "the world turned upside down".

The breakdown of revolutionary hopes and ultimate failure of the Commonwealth experiment forced further re-evaluation. The rule of saints had not occurred, the King was restored and radical groups dissolved, most departing from politics altogether. An age of religious enthusiasm, as it was called (we would use the word fanaticism) had ended, that world subject to the satyr of Samuel Butler who refers to attempts to settle disputes by "the holy text of pike and gun". This is not the place to begin such an exploration, but one can see in late seventeenth-century England interesting conditions and conclusions that led, in time, to the establishment of (greater) toleration. This is not to idealise England over and against France, with respect to their revolutions, merely to argue that there were significant shifts, civil and political, in terms of a *de facto* "tolerance of practical rationality" (Scribner, 2002). This included a stance of effective latitudinarianism (i.e., a refusal to "make windows into people's souls") and new languages of conduct and governing, involving both state and personal government. No wonder, given such changes, that society became more cognisant of the centrality of contractual obligations and trust relations, which had to be established and earned, rather than divine ones (Tully, 1988).

A question of the body

The metaphor of society as body has a long history, including "body politic", church as "body of Christ", monarch as "head" of state, knights as "hands" of state and so on.[1] The analogy was used obsessively during the medieval period. Later, in the era of absolutism, sovereign power is directly embodied in the figure of the monarch, from whom the right to punish derives: "Before the justice of the sovereign, all voices must be still" (Foucault, 1975, p. 36). The body of the monarch symbolised a perfected state. That was the theory, at least.

The language of the body, the corps, is an influential metaphor by which rulers, governments, and states define themselves. And with revolutions come revolutionary subjects and bodies, filled and fleshed out by the conviction of their cause: the fist, the shout, the march, the fraternal embrace, the muscular hero, perfect communist mother, to name a few. Emotions change alongside, hence releasing republican sentiment, revolutionary zeal, puritan self-observation, religious piety, and so forth; virtue, in body and soul, released, creating virtuous bodies, individual and collective (Turner, 2012). In this regard, one might make reference to Robespierre's conception of a "Republic of Virtue" founded on Reason and associated with an aggrandised, self-serving belief system—the Cult of the Supreme Being. The replacement of one world and its symbols by another.

It is useful to ponder over the type of social body that the revolutionaries, of various descriptions, were setting themselves against, and why, in the case of Britain in the seventeenth century and France in the eighteenth, its emblems had to be severed from society; to behead an established ruler carries enormous connotative significance. Where does authority come from and how is it justified? It would be a simplification to say that theories of power mirror its actuality, and the "divine right of kings" is no exception. Notions of delegated, Godly power have a long provenance; like a pyramid, "whatever is found 'below', was derived from 'above' ... 'There is no power but of God'" (Ullmann, 1972). And, in the hand of absolutist monarchs and their ministers, a formula such as *raison d'état* ("reason of state") was used to justify any action. By the Renaissance and beyond, divine right theory was an influential doctrine that had actual, material, and legal effects, as well as considerable contestation (Sharpe & Zwicker, 1998). Jean Bodin, a leading French theorist of absolutism, saw sovereignty as absolute and indivisible, but in practice it was never so. In the divine right theory, as Lynn Hunt (1990, p. 27) explains, "the king was father of his people, and his authority as king was modelled on the authority of fathers in families" and also derives from the Scriptural and classical sources, the familiar notion that the king was God's steward or lieutenant on earth. This confluence of the secular and the sacred, its "naturalisation", made it a powerful doctrine.

The king as the "bright image" of God is commonly presented in early seventeenth-century England (Kiryanova, 2015). A monarch who himself wrote frequently about the nature of, and threats to, rule was James I of England (previously James IV of Scotland); at an address to parliament in 1609 he opines on the nature of *jus divinium,* or divine right, warning that any departure from the king's power and rule constitutes sedition.[2] Of course, what seems like an iron-tight rationale of power in one period is vulnerable in another. The figure of the ideal monarch continued to build in the reign of his successor, Charles I; literally built, as in his accession ceremony and other representations, when large stature and beauty, amongst other features, were emphasised, the physical body being an emblem of supremacy (Kiryanova, 2015). But what stands tall can topple, and divine theory was turned on itself, with Charles I accused as traitor to God. Questioning royal power and its justifications was not exactly new, there being a history of scattered radical movements that would not hesitate to confront "ungodly tyrants", at whatever cost to themselves. Sharpe (Sharpe & Zwicker, 1998, p. 26) argues that one of the failures of the English Revolution was that "the commonwealth failed to produce a viable counter image of the republic", with, indeed, Cromwell borrowing imagery from that of the commanding, warrior king. That being so, and the return of kings notwithstanding, no one should underestimate the importance to history and its symbols of the removal of the king's head from his body. Things were never to be the same again.

Over the channel, French absolutism was equally bodied by doctrines of divine right. The excessive imagery of Louis XIV, the so-called Sun King—and Louis the Great, the Beloved etc.—and the symbolism and splendour of his palace, is well known. During a long and "personal" reign, he is built up in state rituals and celebrated in hundreds of formal portraits and countless statues and medals, buoyed up with wigs and heels. He is first portrayed as the child king, who holds continuity and destiny, and later in his long reign as the man who defies illness (smallpox to name one of many) and aging and who is portrayed as Roman emperor, Alexander the Great, and so forth. In the political structures of the *ancien régime*, the king guarantees the natural order of things (Merrick, 1998). Corporal and cosmological, and familial, metaphors were its superglue.

As was the case in England, so too in France, that iron doctrines were easily returned to their rulers, who could be accused of weakness, fallibility, and of unjust, ungodly conduct. And the other side of the perfect, projected body was the diabolical minister and the monstrous, debased monarch and his acolytes, be they be wives, courtiers, clerics, and so forth. The godly and masculinist imagery that sustained kings was also their undoing.

In his detailed historical research, de Baecque (1993) traces the implosion of such imagery and its replacement by revolutionary alternatives, themes such as the "degeneracy of the nobility, impotence of the king, Herculean strength of citizenry and bleeding hearts of the martyrs" (p. 4). And in the defeat of the body of the king, we see, he argues, "a major caesura or gap in the French system of political representation" (p. 30). There are countless ways in which the body of the king began its descent, began what many historians have referred to as a process of "desacralisation". For example, the many rumours, commentaries, parodies, and visual representations (portraiture, pamphlet, cartoon, etc.; on the interweaving of social change, both gradual and revolutionary, and media, see Briggs & Burke, 2009) effectively nullify the monarch in both physical and moral terms. This included *mauvais discours*, or subversive talk, which, as has been noted, is historically old, even if its meaning varied from era to era. From the powerful upright and potent figure issues another, that of the impotent, reduced, imbecile king. Not only this, but his queen is equally turned upon, viciously, as another enemy of France—perfidious, lascivious, usurping. Her "foreign" nature is an over-determined symbol. The king is represented, sometimes in lurid pornography, as under her sway, a cuckold, with the Queen as man-eater, tiger, hyena, and so forth. And as for the animal and the organic register, Louis is the fatted pig, ox, giant stomach, or vegetable. With their desperate attempt to escape, in the flight to Varennes (1791), any residual majesty associated to the king and queen is finally lost. In this, and many other fantastic narratives, satire and fear, subversion and mockery are all present and active (Botting, 2014). Given the ever-present danger of factions, conspirators, and counter-revolutionaries, the revolutionaries used the image of the hydra (representing monarchy, aristocracy, and so forth)—"The hydra is a distinctive, regenerating sort of monster, which grows a new head if one is severed" (Landes, 2004, p. 155).

Emmanuel Sieyès is the priest-philosopher of the revolution, who is credited with authorising the National Assembly to replace the notion of separate "Estates" (June 1789) and who, at a later stage helped paved the way for Napoleon's *coup d'état* (Rudé, 1964; Sewell, 1994); one could say that the Assembly was the embodiment of a unified mass. Like others, Sieyès used corporal (and other) metaphors to diagnose supposed disease within the social body and its cures. A language of degeneracy is invoked, a social body that is subject to wounds, symptoms, cries, and general loss of vigour, with a plea for regeneration and questions raised as to what is the true basis for the constitution of society. If disease is located within the vice of privilege, then the cure is to break the knot of past abuse and reconstitute society on the basis of a new unity in "[t]he great body of the citizens, natural in its movements, certain in its stride … always in proportion with the soul of virtuous citizens" (Sieyès quoted in de Baecque, 1997, p. 84). The aristocracy, and clerics, became a merciless targets for accusations of monstrosity (greed, excess, indifference to suffering, and so forth), privilege becoming the new sin. In an inspired move, Sieyès nominates the new National Assembly as the centre of that unity and the new colossus. The new man is born—the free man—and a new social body, the republican body, which in turn is characterised as monstrous and unnatural by its many detractors, notably in England by conservative politician Edmund Burke (2006), who denounced the new French "monstrous constitution". The theme of the "desacralised monarchy", or the destruction of religion, have been questioned, or at least qualified, on the grounds that, for example, the revolutionaries at first wanted to replace an absolute monarchy with a constitutional one, but also that new images of divinity associated with the republic followed in time (Doyle, 2000). It hardly needs to be stated that Emperor Napoleon puts himself as the centre and embodiment of the nation—the "citizen emperor", the "people's king"—alongside Josephine who, at his coronation, delivered her oath of loyalty on bended knee (Dwyer, 2015). Natural, masculine power is restored. In related vein, Hunt (1983) has commented on the cultural frames that surround all notions of authority and so societal change can often result in a "crisis of representation". It is one thing to efface the old symbols, quite another to actually create new, let alone viable ones.

In recent times, very different causes dominate, together with struggles of representation. Languages of the body vary enormously and societies continually redefine between proper and improper uses of the body and its pleasures. For example, the "sexual revolutions" of the 1960s witnessed a whole series of articulations and rearticulations of power and discourse and body, which continue to be felt; the judgement of history notwithstanding, it is still the case that "Western countries made gigantic steps forwards in the 1960s with an aperture, upsurge and liberation of sexualities" (Hekma & Giami, 2014, p. 1). There are long historical connections back to eighteenth-century redefinitions of liberty, the scope of pleasure, and utopian dreams of sexual liberation. The story of sexuality as a "civil right" is indeed a deep one. We have seen how the subversive work of print pornographers and writers during the French revolution was a radical challenge to a previous vision of life, and mockery of the sanctified, allegedly puritanical, past. In France and elsewhere, and to differing degrees, what constituted "private space" was redefined, with the Enlightenment creating a host of "new ideas about nature, gender, privacy, identity and writing" (Hekma & Giami, 2014, p. 4). The "libertine" was an admired (albeit it male) figure for many, precisely because of his ability to free sensual life from asceticism. The modern idea of the body as one's sole property—and the corresponding right or freedom to use it as one wishes was gaining ground.

Fear of the people

The origins of crowd theory are to be found in a late nineteen-century cultural mix, as constructed by the speculations of early sociologists, criminologists, and essayists, in France and elsewhere. But it has a prehistory in much earlier political discourses of power, linked to fears of earlier revolutions and of the threat posed by revolutionary ideas, including democracy, and other "levelling" ideas. Indeed, with the social changes unleashed by the French Revolution "the social sciences entered into a problematic relationship with the past" (Reedy, 1994, p. 1), which could no longer be seen as fixed nor preordained.

In the earlier eighteenth century, words such as "sympathy" had largely positive connotations, associated with the operation of emotions between people, with polite society and genteel communication. Simply put, sympathy enabled sociality. But other connotations gained ground that were more critical, were more conservative, connotations associated with disruption and collective contagion. Then came a revolution. "In the aftermath of the French revolution, such collective communication is viewed not as a curiosity but as a threat" (Fairclough, 2013, p. 4). And what more famous expression of this view could there be, in England, but that offered by Edmund Burke's (2006) denunciation of the French upheavals as the "swinish multitude" who were encouraged by the revolution, with all its violation of "natural order".

Space prevents me from tracing some of these shifting views and controversies, but if we fast-forward to some of the late nineteenth-century crowd theorists, we can see how such fears continued to be expressed, dressed this time in an emergent language of social science. There are many correlations between these group theories and feared groups, national decline, and dangerous classes. One of the earliest French theorists, Hippolyte Taine, drawing on a rudimentary evolutionary psychology and sociology, emphasised, la race, le milieu, et le moment (race, environment, and epoch; see van Ginneken, 1992). His work invokes a powerful imagery of the animalistic mob, the hysterical crowd, and threat of societal regression; the abortive revolution of 1871, the Commune, but also other expressions of unrest, reinforced those fears, for Taine and for others.

The unruly crowd and passionate mob, then, were the phenomenon on which subsequent thinkers, such as Le Bon, Tarde, and others, constructed notions of contagion, suggestibility, and primitive behaviour. The crowd was itself theorised during a revolutionary era and such thinkers encapsulated many of the fears of their well-to-do contemporaries: "Their crowds loomed as violent, bestial, insane, capricious beings whose comportment resembled that of the mentally-ill, women, alcoholics, or savages" (Burrows, 1981, p. 5). Burrows identifies a notable misogynistic strand in Le Bon's theory, with woman as symbolic of instability, suggestibility, and emotion, the same qualities he ascribes to crowds. On the other hand, Le Bon also drew on a register of masculine denigration in his portrayal of the crowd, in which he spoke of its brutality, force, and destruction (Borch, 2012). Others theorists contributed, in France and elsewhere, with their allied interests in the anthropological (e.g., "race" and human "types") and the criminological (e.g., the "degenerate" and "criminal mob"). Le Bon in particular draws upon the *cultural refs. come thick & fast & are dizzying in their multiplicity.*

realms of psychopathology and suggestion to develop his semi-popular, semi-scientific treatise on the crowd. Nye (1995), in his introduction to an edition of Le Bon's treatise, rightly notes that Le Bon was a member of the old elite and that the advice he proffers was intended for the use of sober statesmen. The socialist revolutionary crowds were believed to represent a mortal risk to civilisation itself.

Conclusion

Revolution and revolutionary change are not easy to define, even if they carry connotations of a radical breakthrough, a fundamental revision, a break, and a turning-around of events. Even so, such changes are not always as sudden as at first they may appear, and often we judge an outcome "revolutionary" by means of a retrospective assessment, though sometimes it is apparent overnight, as it were. In whatever way, however, "the revolutionary" event changes the constitution of available narratives by shaking up the world and creating new ones. In this way, things are never quite the same again.

This chapter has touched upon the rich imagery and narratives of revolution, its demands and bodies, and, also, how fear of revolution promoted some of the first formalised theories of crowd and group behaviour.

Notes

1. For some illuminating essays on the theme of body politic and contemporary nationalisms or racism, see Auestad (2014).
2. James I wrote a notorious treatise on demonology and not only encouraged but presided over the some of the Scottish witch trials; later, in England, his interest in such matters waned. This interest, however, was consistent with his insistence on defining the integrity of the state and of absolute natures of kingly power (Borman, 2014; Larner, 1984). I have argued (Weegmann, 2014b) that in this and other influential continental texts on witchcraft, the worse form of malignant "rebellion" was located in the vile body of the witch, who, in the language of the Old Testament (of course, James authorised the King James version of the Bible, 1611), should not be "suffered to live". The very integrity of the world, with its legion inner enemies, was at stake.

CHAPTER SIX

Psychoanalytic fascinations: my seven Freuds ... .

I n this semi-formal, part-autobiographical chapter, I offer a number of critical reflections on the theme of my relationship to Freud and psychoanalysis. Beyond this, I touch upon the subject of fascination, be it to persons or to movements and the ideals they carry, including those of the psychoanalytic movement itself. I trace some of the theoretical currents that have influenced my thinking since the late 1970s, such as feminism, Foucault, and literary criticism, and touch upon my formation as clinical psychologist and group analyst. I advocate the importance of maintaining a critical discourse about psychoanalysis (in its many faces), which continues to have influence far beyond the clinical world.

Freud at first sight

I bought my first (Pelican paperback) Freud book at sixteen in a grubby, anarchist bookshop near to Leeds University in 1973 It was the *New Introductory Lectures on Psycho-Analysis* (1933a) and cost 35p. Two things stuck me on reading Strachey's life sketch of Freud and the contents of the book, one being the question of why Hitler burned Freud's books—actually in the same year as the lectures were published—and the second the dazzling, dense disconcertion of his topics. As for the former, I pondered on the nature of the hatred that could regard a mere book as a threat. And as for the latter, nothing prepared me for a book dealing with dreams, neurosis, instinctual life, childhood complexes, and femininity, all within 200-odd pages. It was a new world and a vocabulary that I could compare to nothing, read with a mixture of fascination and apprehension, given the proximity of its concerns to the adolescent anxieties of its reader. It was like discovering gold wrapped with a personal warning: "Be careful where this might point". Consuming the book with fiery enthusiasm, there were two other issues. The first was financial, in that I now wanted volume one, *The Introductory Lectures* of 1915, and Freud's biography, and, what with the train fare and all, it was a stretch on my pocket. The second concern was where to hide them, as I was afraid my parents would find them. I buried them at the back of a chest of drawers, wrapped in socks and vests, thinking that the strange agency Freud called the "super-ego" was definitely what my parents had, not realising I had "one" too. A few more psychology books came to nestle amongst the socks, and then another book fit for burning or banning—*The Communist Manifesto*. Friends subsequently observed that they were my "dirty books". Yes, in the case of Freud, maybe so, but in the case of Marx, it was more a case of "dangerous knowledge".

I dreamed (of the daytime variety) of becoming a "child analyst". I should explain that my first love, in primary school, was archaeology, and so, when this waned, the psychic excavations of Freud were attractive, with their journey into the deepest layers of the unknown mind. Aiming my sights on that profession, I wrote off to various training institutes (I've no idea how I found them out) to ask for information on how to proceed. I received responses from the Anna Freud Centre, possibly The Institute of Psychoanalysis, and Margaret Lowenfelt's Institute of Child Psychology (now closed; I gather her approach was more eclectic than psychoanalytic), with leaflets and kindly letters suggesting that I should first concentrate on A levels. Of course, I had no real idea what a child analyst did, except that it seemed to involve clever experts breaking the codes so as to gain access to little unconscious minds.

The first clinical text of Freud that I bought was the almost Victorian and Promethean *Studies in Hysteria*. The Gothic genre, with its dark forces, divided minds, and deviations might have coloured my reading, since around the same time I saw a grainy black and white TV version of *Jekyll and Hyde,* although I do not know which I came upon first. Stevenson prefixed his famous novella with the words, "The strange case of ...", and Freud's pursuit of the "case study", expounded as a systematic unfolding, drew me in. The expressions coined by his patients, such as "talking cure" and "chimney sweeping", added to the mystique, as did the image of the penetrating analyst. The *Studies* unnerved me, for if late nineteenth-century hysterics had unconscious problems, what might it also have to say about my "dark half"? My repressions? Questions that troubled me.

My Freud at first sight was (age-appropriately) naive and was, I suppose, a beginner's version of the intrepid Freud legend. I liked the Ernest Jones's loyal, royal biography, and Freud's self-image as conquistador, opening up new vistas of psychic life. If psychoanalysis was an "embattled science", that made it all the more interesting. It was love at first sight.

Whilst studying developmental psychology at the University of Sussex in the late 1970s, I encountered hostility or bemused indifference towards Freud. Most seemed to regard psychoanalysis as little more than a museum piece or curio. I met smiling tolerance and an implied "forget about it"; psychology, it was said, had "moved on". Modern psychology did not need bonfires, and indifference was more effective at extinguishing interest. Lecturers simply had no place for him on their cognitive maps (this was during a time when Piaget was making the headlines, some hailing him as the saviour of scientific psychology). There was one exception—Professor Marie Jahoda—who gave a splendid address on Freud, with Viennese accent to go with it, and whom I later discovered was a lifelong socialist and visionary social psychologist. Unfortunately it was a one-off visit, as she had retired from the university.

The more I read, the more convinced I was that the hostility and non-recognition of Freud must be based on myths and was little more than a continuation of the kinds of rejection that Freud had himself suffered. In the arrogance of a premature conclusion, I believed they had not read him properly—my prompt to enter the circle of the embattled, as it was reassuring to have enemies. There is a passage in the *New Introductory Lectures* (1933a, p. 139) where Freud states: "There is a common saying that we should learn from our enemies. I confess I have never succeeded in doing so". Quite!

There were more than a few refugees from developmental psychology, the disillusioned who sought solace in other regions, including bars, a change of degree, a few in the anti-psychiatry of Laing. Chance had it that I was advised to consult with literature departments who were, allegedly, more sympathetic to Freud than the psychologists. And so it was that I knocked, nervously, on the door of a lecturer, Dr. Jacqueline Rose, who gave me two papers to assist in the fight—"Critical empiricism criticised" (Cosin, Freeman & Freeman, 1971), which helped me counter the popular positivist dismissals of Freud, and Laplanche and Leclaire's (1972) "The unconscious: a psychoanalytic study", which brought a mysterious newcomer, Lacan, to my attention. Dr. Rose was confident, even visionary, and that emboldened me. The French were coming.

Political Freud

Lacan was an important bridge towards an acceptable, "political" view of psychoanalysis. I say acceptable, because as a budding Marxist, soon to join the Communist Party, it was essential to find views that fitted a radical project whilst transcending the bourgeois ideology that I saw as dominating the whole of developmental psychology. Piaget was no aid to any revolutionary cause, and his books as dry as bone. I searched for whatever I could of Lacan translated into English, and read Anika Lemaire's (1979) fine introduction, thinking that in Lacan's "return to Freud" and "unconscious structured like a language" there was the reading to replace all others, which could provide ammunition in the trench warfare I was mounting with academic psychology. Lacan began to pop up in my essays, to the confusion of tutors. I was aided by another French giant, Louis Althusser, and his wonderful essay (1971), "Freud and Lacan". It remains a brilliant read, entirely assertive, and, in its time, was an "intervention" on behalf of psychoanalysis, which had been condemned in the French Communist Party as a reactionary ideology. Althusser sought detent. As for me, revolutionary causes required a revolutionary theory of subjectivity, and Freud, via Lacan, via Althusser, seemed to supply it.

Althusser starts lyrically with a birth story, saying that "the nineteenth century saw the birth of two or three children that were not expected: Marx, Nietzsche and Freud" (p. 182) and claims that Freud worked in theoretical solitude, running his own business, being his own father. That he placed Freud next to Marx was a good sign, and the mighty Nietzsche too, who had been a sixth-form hero. Althusser proceeds to rescue Freud from the various "reductionisms" with which he is associated, whether it be biological stages of development (the dreaded crime of "biologism"), the childhood past (the simplistic error of "psychologism"), and what we clumsily called a "sociologised" version of psychoanalysis. I was not alone in searching for a version of Freud that could replace his language of instincts and libidinous energy with a new language, such as those of signifiers, symbolic orders, imaginaries, desires, and so forth. I could tell the teachers that they had him all wrong and that I had *the* reading of Freud, the "symptomatic reading" that broke surface understanding. The true objects of psychoanalysis were delivered in quotable punches—Althusser again: "One of the 'effects' of the humanization of the small biological creature that results from human parturition: there in its place is the object of psychoanalysis, an object which has a simple name; '*the unconscious*'" (op. cit., p. 189). The human subject is a decentred subject.

In a final flourish, Althusser endorses Lacan's use of structural linguistics. Through the operation of the Symbolic, we face a forced march that transforms "mammiferous larvae into human children, *masculine* or *feminine subjects*" (p. 190). Such laws of culture demand further investigation, a task that Althusser delegates to "historical materialism". So we are back to Marx and all is well. Psychoanalysis and Marxism rehabilitated. For a brief while anyway.

I am glad I spent the time seeking a political Freud, even if reading, like socialism, took up a lot of evenings. Since then, I see that psychoanalysis easily *occludes* the function of power in relationships (and therapy) and has often been transformed into a "liberal theory of adjustment", as Fromm (1982) puts it. Anthropologist Mary Douglas (1970, p. 90) observes of psychoanalysis, that it takes into account only a limited social field, making "parents and siblings the social framework into which all subsequent relationships are slotted. The restriction gives it great theoretical elegance and power". Unfortunately, it also gives it a loss of sight, even though debates continue as to the radical versus conservative nature of psychoanalysis (Elliot, 2002).

Some would argue that psychoanalysis helps us to better understand the investments with(in) oppression and the affective identifications that attract and define our positions; we both seek change and fear it. Equally, there is what McDougall (1977) calls a strong "normopathic strand" at the heart of psychoanalysis. Looking back, and for all his brevity and rhetorical flourish, Althusser's touching on language, desire, and sexual difference opened another door for me, equally linked to politics, but of another kind—feminism. And it was to psychoanalytic feminism that I turned—another rapprochement perhaps—although many disagreed, often vehemently. My fellow communist comrades at Sussex spoke of the need to "live socialism", but the male-dominated Left were being kicked where it hurt by the feminist movement. The personal was indeed political, but not in the safe and controlled way that many socialists had previously reckoned.

Feminist Freud

The Marxism that seemed so alive and vital in the 1970s ran out of steam. Marxism was never equal in any of its relationships and wanted psychoanalysis, as well as "the women's issue", as some traditional comrades patronisingly put it, on its terms, rather than as a proper engagement. I had by this time left the Communist Party (around 1981) and socialist intellectuals generally were on the defensive, not only due to electoral realities, but by wave after wave of feminist criticism (Rowbotham, Segal & Wainwright, 1979). The male Left had a roasting, although not everyone came out cooked. Subjectivity mattered again and was no longer seen as a reactionary digression from something more important, nor was it the "effect" of some structure. And so it was in feminism that I found a more productive, yet still radical reappraisal of Freud.

Debates and exchanges between feminism and psychoanalysis have raged for years. There were some points on which everyone could agree that Freud got it wrong—penis envy, the traditional oedipal scheme, the suggestion (although itself much contested) that "anatomy is destiny", and so on. Further, psychoanalysis often did reduce all "to a family paradigm" (Gallop, 1982, p. 144). Juliet Mitchell's *Psychoanalysis and Feminism* (1974) was a clarification and corrective to the earlier tradition of feminist criticism of Freud. I found the enigmatic journal *M/F* inspiring if schematic and not an easy read, but I derived borrowed strength from the curt editorials and theoretical interrogations, including their liberal use of the words of the times—discourse/discursive.

Rediscovering Jacqueline Rose (1978, 1983), I found what I thought was the formula for a real appreciation of complex psychic reality, that drew upon the feminist project. There was still something that seemed exceptional about psychoanalytic discourse and it was her emphasis on resistance and non-identity that drew my interest. Rose says: "The unconscious constantly reveals the 'failure' of identity. Because there is no continuity of psychic life, so there is no stability of sexual identity, no position for women (or for men) which is ever simply achieved" (1983, p. 9). Furthermore, she continues, "failure" is not something to be regretted, but something "endlessly repeated and relived moment for moment throughout our individual histories" (op. cit). With resistance then at/in the heart of our identity, or lack of it, Freud's young hysteric, Dora, was, for me and others, a revalued heroine of the literature. The patient was fighting back.

Dora is possibly the most read of Freud's cases. Why, is not difficult to discern—she was, after all, an eighteen-year-old female treated by a forty-four-year-old man, who used her "case", or a fragment of it, to establish a revolutionary new therapy. Unlike the *Studies*, where Freud and Breuer use physical pressure, catharsis, and only an embryonic free association, being on the cusp of Freud's major theoretical discoveries, the Dora case illustrates a young psychoanalysis, confident with free association and the analysis of dreams. Much has been made of the dubious "exchange" that comes into the treatment, with Dora as pawn in a wider power game. Further, is she expected to fall into the new narrative of Freud or does she express her own and ultimately spurn the analyst by breaking off? Both have strong willpower. Gilmore (1994) considers this narrative struggle from a feminist viewpoint and underlines Freud's anxiety about his case appearing in the public domain: "I naturally cannot prevent the patient herself from being pained if her own case history should accidentally fall into her hands" (Freud, 1905e, pp. 8–9). Gilmore refers to the process by which Freud sought clinical and theoretical legitimacy through the cases that will found his science, as with Dora and the veritable battle between "his" narrative assertions and "hers". No one lies quietly on the couch, but the reasons for resistance are not always quite as the psychoanalyst diagnoses them. Dora finished with Freud, but he continued to struggle with her, *in absentia*, in his effort to secure firm foundations for the practice of psychoanalysis (Marcus, 1981).

Of no less interest in such connections is the less celebrated case of Freud's (1920a) anonymous female homosexual, whom he calls "the girl". With parallels to the Dora scenario, "the girl" attends as part of a family "referral", where, as a result of a disapproved and proscribed attachment to another female, and rejection of a "speedy marriage" to resolve it, her father's only other option is to turn to psychoanalysis. In some ways Freud is radical, refusing to take things at first hand and not seeing her sexual orientation per se as problematic: "she did not suffer from anything in herself, nor did she complain of her condition" (Freud, 1920, p. 150). Having agreed to see her, he suggests to the parents that he can only "study" her for a while in order to see whether she might be amenable to analysis proper. Freud soon concludes that this second stage is not possible and so discharges her, although it is unclear whether she is a push-out or drop-out. He appears angry, either in response to her defiance and/or because of her cool detachment from the analytic process—"*la belle indifférence*" as he puts it, but, in this respect, she mimics the "studying" analyst (Forrester & Appignanesi, 2001). In spite of the radical dimension, there is also the Freud who is convinced that he understands the real libidinal sources of her development and so, retrospectively, leaves the reader in no doubt about his formulation of the psychogenesis behind her "turning away from men".

In recent years there has been a burgeoning of gay/lesbian study excavating the traces and presence of homophobia in psychoanalysis, with the 1920 case illustrative of blind spots in Freud's viewpoint (Lesser Schoenberg, 1999). "The girl" represents an unsettling of all that was and was not expected of educated females in the Vienna of those times and her indifference a challenge to the confident, libidinal theories of the psychoanalyst, however "liberal" his then viewpoint might have been.

Textual Freud

Around 1982 I engaged in some modest Freud-tourism, visiting Berggasse 19 in Vienna, the newly opened Freud Museum in London, and even dropping in, without appointment, to the Salpêtrière Hospital in Paris, where I saw some of Charcot's famous photographs of hysterics. Homage is a component of fascination, proximity being the critical factor, closeness to a valued and hallowed person, place, or movement. It was also in Paris that I jealously eyed the *Standard Edition of the Complete Psychological Works of Sigmund Freud* in a bookshop and resolved to study him with renewed rigour on my return, which meant looking beyond my tatty *Pelican* paperbacks. Fortunately help arrived in the form of an offer by Jill Duncan, the then librarian at the Institute of Psychoanalysis, to access their impressive stock. Once a week I would spend an evening there, reading Freud and whoever else distracted me.

This was a time of Derrida-mania and "consulting the text" was considered important. If Freud was to be read, then he had to be read closely, microscopically. Footnotes mattered, sometimes more so than the main body of the text, as they illustrated Freud's slippages, supplements, retrospective wisdom. But unlike Lacan's mystical motif of "return", now there was no essential text at all. Play, pun, and irreverence were seriously important, and one read between the lines, backwards, from late Freud to early Freud, and sideways through minor as much as major texts. Some would call it obsessive, but I was entranced. I guess it was consistent with a certain "cult of difficulty"—the more difficult, or obscure, the better. I vowed to write a book, entitled "Ambivalences of Psychoanalysis", but it remained unfinished. More importantly, I had started personal psychotherapy, my therapist pointing out that I was disappointed that in spite of all my heady knowledge of Freud and Co, I was still in need of help.

One book that spoke to my "textual phase" was Samuel Webber's *The Legend of Freud* (1982) with its emphasis on "the participation of psychoanalysis in the dislocations it seeks to describe". I was drawn by his reading that played around with internal contradictions of the Freudian corpus and in how "the text" always exceeded the intentions and professed aims of the author. Consistent with the displacement of consciousness-as-central, Freud too was decentred and thus assessed independently of the "legend" he helped create. There are two meanings of the word "legend", one of which indicates the fabulous, the tale, and the other which signifies marginal inscriptions on coins, maps, etc. Weber deals with both meanings—Freud as legendary, mesmeric figure, and "Freud" as the proper name assigned to his texts. Frank Sulloway (1979), in a very different sort of way, deconstructs and qualifies the heroic Freud legend. If the author is not quite dead, then at least he/she should have some of their stuffing and pretentions taken out.

A literary Freud

"I invented psychoanalysis because it had no literature", joked Freud (cited in Roazen, 1969, p. 92).

One cannot read Freud and not be taken by his prose; it is supremely enjoyable, compelling (Phillips, 2006). Good writers dazzle. No mere secondary matter of expression, Freud's manner of writing is bound to the writing and traditions that influenced him, his effort to create a new discourse, and need to convince the reader; rhetoric, claim, and reality flow together, as he wards off potential criticism and defends his science. The *Introductory Lectures* are a majestic example of this, as in addressing his "Ladies and Gentlemen" Freud continually envisages objections, which he seeks to answer. Brandell (1979) sees links between Freud and the "depth-psychology oriented literature of the turn of the century" (p. xi). And the influence goes both ways. Addressing the British context, Hinshelwood (1995) argues that literature was one influential "point of cultural access" for psychoanalysis.

Frank Sulloway's (1992) excellent contribution on the construction of psychoanalysis as practice and organisation considers Freud's manner of writing and address. Known mainly for his exploration of Freud's biology—"biologist of the mind"—Sulloway considers Freud's preoccupation with the dissemination of the psychoanalytic mode of knowledge. In this respect the case studies (cases that are still studied in contemporary institutes) have a special status, intended to explicate and educate at the same time. They were privileged texts, with other analysts soon adding to the tradition of the "case report". Sulloway (1992, p. 175) refers to a "literary technology" and rhetorical strategy: "[l]ike the patient, the reader is subjected to a psychoanalytic 'education'". This links with Freud's "social technology", referring to the manner in which he conducted himself and constructed his movement, "wielding the bulk of his power in the service of what he called 'the cause'" (op. cit., p. 181). Once theoretical claims and their "findings" are repeated successively, it is easy to see how analytic observations become transformed into facts, "interprefactions", to use the term coined by Borch-Jacobsen and Shamdasani (2008).

Supervisors and role models

As a young clinical psychologist I described myself, brusquely, as "psychoanalytic", a badge of distinction. Words can seal power and how people self-nominate is revealing. For me, in a clinical psychology context, "psychoanalytic" was much firmer than the softer "psychodynamic" that some used, and which, nowadays, I prefer as one amongst a range of professional self-descriptions. During clinical psychology training I went for gold, seeking a placement in a psychoanalytic child and family department. Klein and Bion were central points of reference, for me new figures of interest accompanied by a whole new lexicon of "the infant". If Freud had taken me to the well of psychic archaeology, Klein showed me deep geology. I attended lectures by Hanna Segal, who was fond of using the "pure wine" metaphor of psychoanalysis, contrasted no doubt by its watered-down substitutes. Such confident, congratulatory representations are deeply embedded in psychoanalysis, as in Freud's (1919h) contrasting of the "pure gold of analysis" from the "copper of direct suggestion" in other psychotherapies; increasingly, what marked psychoanalysis was the role of interpretation, of resistance, and the transference. I was, in Segal's asides, and throughout my time on placement, pulled by a powerful shared identification with an elevated, heroic version of psychoanalysis. One of the questions I was asked on placement—paradoxically given the fact that I was already a trainee—was, "Are you thinking of going on to do a training?", a metonym for the Institute of Psychoanalysis. All roads lead to ...?

While I knew about group identification in theory, and how it played out in the history of the psychoanalytic movement, it was revealing, and discomforting, to see how it worked there, in the clinic, in front of me. Various styles, conventions, and basic assumptions permeated their practice, including the conduct of case seminars. And humour also. Staff in-jokes are telling in their promotion of group solidarity. The "opposition", including most of the approaches used by my fellow psychology trainees, were often subject to psychoanalytic diagnosis; one declared that cognitive therapy was a "manic defence", and another dismissed behavioural approaches as quite "mad". I heard it said that children with attentional difficulties were "expert at attacks on linking" and that autism was a form of infantile psychosis. The parents of the children were at best regarded as supporting actors to the "real work" that was going on elsewhere, between the child and his or her therapist. Phantasy was to the forefront, the transference and countertransference working-through considered the mutative agents; there was scant talk of the impact of deprived estates, single parents, patterns of learning, and the like. Unfortunately I internalised this rather imperial stance, including the superior humour, and applied it liberally. All played a part in shoring up a "newly qualified" professional identity.

I had the privilege of learning from several psychoanalysts once qualified. True to form I regarded their supervision as being of a different order to that of psychologists, which I saw as mundane. Arrogance and idealisation notwithstanding, I learned a great deal from them and they became role models. What struck me, and what I sought as a quality, was just how "in command" they seemed, unperturbed, beyond surprise. That was the image at least. They seemed able to see through "the material" quickly, from a distance, and could deliver accurate-sounding observations about what "the patient" was saying. The interpretive scope was applied to other departments as well, elsewhere in the hospital. So I wanted what they had, their assured microscopic and long-distance vision.

Looking back, I discovered the obvious—that psychoanalysts have professional selves to defend and can carry common prejudices, invariably not seen at the time. I am glad that I had thoughtful supervision, but gladder that I eventually allowed psychology colleagues to temper and moderate my stripped-down and stern psychoanalytic leanings.

A group-analyst's Freud

I did not read much Freud during group-analytic training (1998–2002), but was interested in the relationship of psychoanalysis and group analysis, explored in more detail in the final chapter. Foulkes was a loyal Freudian (trained in the Anna Freud, or "B" school) whilst developing a theory and practice quite different, or at least in parallel, to the psychoanalysis he continued to practice. In terms of his early identification, Foulkes sought Freud as his analyst of choice, although settled, along with his then wife, in a curious twin analysis, with Helene Deutsch. He had to be satisfied with a one-off meeting with the Professor (on 12 August 1936 at 11.30 a.m.). Foulkes (1969a) describes Freud's dignity, and his unusual combination of the stilted and relaxed. Freud relates an in-joke when he asks Foulkes about how he finds the climate (*Klima*) in London, an oblique reference to the growing influence of Melanie Klein. Foulkes is non-committal, pretending literality, but Freud continues making exaggerated "Brrr" gesticulations. Psychoanalysts, or at least one, having fun.

I learned about the historical matrix of psychoanalysis, and Malcolm Pines helped, with his historical knowledge. *Why* did it arise? *Why then?* Why *there?* How did psychoanalysis come to the fore, the singular parent (Althusser's "being your own father"), whilst spawning and spurning various others, including the "step-children" of Moreno's psychodrama and Foulkes' group analysis? (Pines, 1988, 1991). Questions of ownership and who to include within the preeminent analytic family were of great importance during those formative times. Pines draws attention to the radical, socialist Adler who, with his emphasis on social instincts, could be regarded as conceptually close to Foulkes' emphasis on the social nature of being. Foulkes avoided controversy and effectively settled on the comfortable compromise that psychoanalysis and group analysis offered a vertical and a horizontal perspective respectively. Depth enjoined breadth and in an equal division of labour, saves the marriage.

Freud's (1921c) book on group psychology stands alone as a classic, attempting to explain the binding effects and functionality of groups. Freud concentrates on the "artificial" groups of church and army (what is not an artificial group?) and how individual members come to share and identify with a common abstract ideal. The common ideal stands in the place of a specific leader. He noted the multiplicity of groups that influence the individual, and how "he is bound by ties of identification in many directions, and he has built up his own ego ideal upon the most various models" (p. 129). But another place where such study could aptly be applied is the psychoanalytic institute. Psychoanalytic idealisations, schisms, hero construction, and institutional transmission serve a reassuring function—"The condemnation of heresy implies the affirmation of orthodoxy" (Weber, 1982, p. 8). Eisold (1994) argues that intolerance of diverse points of view within psychoanalytic trainings have unfortunately come to constitute formidable "institutional social defences".

I found it disappointing that Foulkes did not draw on group theory to cast new light on the psychoanalytic movement of which he was a part—a sort of group analysis of psychoanalysis. Would this have been a bridge too far? After all, Foulkes began, and ended, with a position of loyalty—"The present writers stand firmly on the grounds of classical psychoanalysis …" (Foulkes & Anthony, 1957, p. 16).

Foucault's Freud

Foucault's research captivated me from University days and ever since, one book after another. When he first addressed psychoanalysis

Bookish!! Fox vs. hedgehog.

in detail, in *The History of Sexuality, Volume 1*, I was intrigued by what he would have to say. Foucault defies classification, being neither just historian, philosopher, nor social theorist per se. Foucault offers a genealogical analysis, including some all too brief observations on the nature of the psychoanalytic quest into human interior life. Foucault does not rob Freud of his originality, but places him in relief. Foucault (rather like Althusser) refers to Freud alongside other notables, as a "founder of discursivity", but is, however, concerned with what makes its emergence as a discipline possible. The term *implication* might help to conceptualise the contexts of psychoanalysis, since etymologically this means something like "being folded within", within cultural loca- tions, new forms of knowledge, and the likes. Wisely, Stern (1996, p. 290) observes, "Psychoanalysts are defined by their culture no less than are the maladies of their patients and—coming full circle—the values that underlie their theories of therapeutic action". In this regard, psy- choanalysis is certainly "vulnerable to its history" (Borch-Jacobsen & Shamdasani, 2012).

In an early work, Foucault (1973) details the formation of clinical medicine and concepts of disease, calling his approach "an archaeology of medical perception". Complex changes in the relationship between "help" and "knowledge" are chartered, in this case the reorganisation of the hospital or clinical field, a new idea of the patient in society, and the development of a relation between public assistance, political needs, and medical experience. Foucault uses the term "gaze" to describe the evolution of these different acts of seeing and intervening, of organising observations. Although his early books were directed at medicine and psychiatry, the ideas can be linked up with his later work that excavates the field of sexuality and the creation of the listening/talking cure that was psychoanalysis. The psychoanalyst came to operate within a par- ticular field of view, possesses an "analytic gaze", and, with a "seeing ear" systematically makes sense of an intricate interior realm, that of an individual's unconscious mind.

Foucault makes much of the "confession" as an analogy for psycho- analysis. He notes (1979, p. 59), "We have become a singularly con- fessing society". The analytic subject is implored to speak (at length, exhaustively, without conscious censure) and through stumbling (slips, inner resistance, and evasion), reveals what is hidden, that which resists its own telling. The analyst has a hermeneutic role in interpreting, deci- phering, seeing signs. In psychoanalysis, the confessional relationship became an instrument in itself, "the work of producing the truth was obliged to pass through this relationship" (Foucault, 1979, p. 66). He links it to the suffering person and the injunction to speak, of looking inwards and backwards to discern those secret principles that govern being. Forrester (1980, p. 290) notes, "in giving birth to the individual, professionals of man installed a truth within him, as the secret core of his being—his sexuality." Or, that was the psychoanalysis as was and Foucault rightly reminds us of the imbrications of Freud's work within the sexology of the era, which, while transforming its terms, is also limited by them. One hundred years on the landscape is quite different. Inner words have replaced instinctual life. Some argue that "attachment" has replaced sex as the central term. Or that the "relational" has supplanted a traditional, hierarchical analyst/patient dynamic. There are many variants on this theme, hardly surprising after a century of psychoanalysis.

Is Foucault's emphasis on "confession" merely the clever use of an analogy that tells us little about the actual structure and claims of psychoanalytic discourse (Cousins & Hussain, 1984)? Is there a lack of specific evidence in Foucault's thesis? However one decides, I think there are definite illuminations in placing psychoanalysis within the broader confessional context of modern society. And once psychoanalysis was on the stage, nothing was quite the same again.

Fascinations

What happens to heroes and heroines? Often they are quietly dropped and melt away with an incoming new interest. For adolescents they assist the development of more formal, abstract reasoning, but usually have their day. Fixations are loosened. Others have a way of staying around, even if the relationship with them changes. Young adults still need supports. Modified perhaps, some may even become lifelong companions. Whilst there is a risk that they become obsolete and block our progress, there is the possibility of a more realistic celebration of what they mean to us, which brings them to size—post-heroes and post-heroines. I think of my "Freud" nowadays as a kind of elderly companion. I do not see him now, indeed usually forget he is there, yet I appreciate all he has represented over time.

A word or two more about fascination. Is there much difference between, say, the cult of celebrity and the elevation of psychoanalytic figures? Are academic or professional idealisations any different to those in other domains? As fascination is a group as much as individual process, groups too are surrounded with symbols, sustaining ideals, and so forth, what Kohut (1981) describes as "cultural selfobjects". Psychoanalysis has its fair share of "aura" effects and charismatic, sometimes oracular, authorities, whose very quotation can replace further thinking. The history of psychoanalysis has witnessed a succession of heroes and heroines and also an unfortunate tendency for truths and great persons to be linked, "the one true test of legitimacy" (Goldberg, 1990, p. 6). There is something appropriately adolescent and young-adultish about fascination, as we fix upon our preferred images and activities; they cause no harm, at least the pro-social ones do not. The images and activities seem "ours" for the owning and we enjoy the simplification of the world that they afford. A hero, a party, a movement, or a band, offer uplifting identification, even (mild) addiction. It also touches upon a less prominent psychoanalytic notion, that of the ego-ideal, although Freud (characteristically) only locates the sources for this in childhood, rather than the contemporaneous groups that surround and influence us. Sheer enjoyment is a factor, as we learn to "use" our chosen object or figure. When I bought my first Freud, even his image on the front cover warmed me to a figure who was wise, deep, and different. As I read him I was lured by a certain omnipotence of vision, a way of seemingly explaining everything going on within us. Freud's psychoanalysis was nothing if it was not comprehensive. Not only this, but the assured self-image that only psychoanalysis deals with the "unconscious depths", whilst other approaches paddle about in the "empirical shallows", continues (Crews, 2006). That image does have a social impact; Moscovoci's (2007, p. 244) exploration of attitudes towards psychoanalysts (in France), claims that during a certain era "they had style, authority and charisma, and thought they had a universal intellectual stature".

Fascination implies a degree of submission, as we "give ourselves over" to someone or something. To dazzle, to charm, to capture, to be captured. Freud spoke of a temporary paralysis of our critical faculties, and speculated about the relationship of hypnotist and hypnotised, and certain forms of love devotion. The topic of fascination comes up again in his group paper. Idealisation is its close cousin, that tendency to overvalue an object, person, or experience. And idealisation includes theories, which Roustang (1976) writes about, and its links to discipleship and transmission in psychoanalytic communities. Be careful with such authority, as tradition and treachery or betrayal are close associates (Spurling, 1993).

As for me, the psychoanalytic vision seemed to offer something complete, a commanding gaze, the "revolutionary excitement" of a discovery that saw beyond the superficial centre to a region of powerful, irrational drama (Frosh, 1997, p. 91). As such, it was more imaginative (seeming) than what I encountered in academic psychology (I subsequently made friends with Piaget, who when all is said and done created a brilliant revolution of his own in developmental psychology and constructivism).[1] Blushes aside, in my psychoanalytic journeys, I too wanted to be deep and wise, and the more "difficult" the path, the more attractive it was, especially if I was on the side of those "in the know". In terms of group identification, I wanted a good seat within the stadium of the intellectual Left, amongst those at home with their ("re-read") Freud and their ("advanced") Marxism. Virtuosos were required, particularly French ones. Later, as clinician, I wanted a good place within the arena of practice that featured my esteemed psychoanalytic colleagues. Fascination has a dual aspect, involving awe and fear in the presence of something or someone who is highly valued. The fear aspect was definitely present, a compensation for feelings of smallness and for actually limited clinical experience.

Writing this chapter proved therapeutic, in so far as it gave me the opportunity to look back whilst catching up, and to speculate on the role that fascinations play within our professional and personal formations. We all need heroines and heroes. But, if fascination fails to move with experience, and if we do not grow up and grow out, then fascination verges on obsession, dogma, or worse.

I lost my fascination in Freud and psychoanalysis, replaced by what I hope is a more mature appreciation of its insights and spirit of inquiry. No longer do I believe that it covers all the territory, far from it, or contains all the references to that which is "deep" within us. Winnicott (1962, p. 239; his target was Klein), said that "deeper in psychology does not always mean earlier", and I would agree. Moreover, importantly, psychoanalysis (and other therapies, including psychology) requires its own reparations on behalf of all those who were *not* served well by it, certainly in the past: victims of sexual abuse who were misdirected into exploring realms of oedipal fantasy, gay men and lesbians held to be developmentally incomplete or hindered, those with substance misuse, or psychosis, hardly assisted in their suffering by (guilt-provoking) relentless interpretation of destructiveness, and so forth. I have encountered many examples, but not only of old. New controversy has recently arisen in France, with the making of documentary, *The Wall*, on autism, and the influence of mistaken views by psychoanalysts working with such individuals, who tried to block its showing. The analysts, for their part, fear being demonised but, in my view, have for too long immunised themselves from wider evidence whilst holding tight to what becomes a self-admiring, problematic heritage. I am including self-reparation in this, for my excesses. You see, I hope my fascination was cured by something more lasting and serviceable—curiosity—which, fortunately, was also there throughout.

Note

1. Piaget (1973) wrote an interesting article, for a psychoanalytic journal, "The affective unconscious and the cognitive unconscious", saying, "I am persuaded that a day will come when the psychology of cognitive functions and psychoanalysis will have to fuse in a general theory which will improve both, through mutual correction." I continue to find his constructivist emphasis on assimilation and accommodation invaluable.

CHAPTER SEVEN

Discipline anxiety—time for paradigm change in group analysis?

This chapter argues that the founding paradigm and dependencies of group analysis are exhausted and that as a therapy its minimal influence, particularly in the public sector but also the private, creates a serious issue of stagnation. In response to these theoretical limitations and declining influence, we could take a road of retreat and isolation, but that will only compound the problem. Alternatively, we can embrace the need for profound paradigm change, and draw sustenance upon new sources and disciplines, so as to better engage with the world as it is now. I shall confine my comments to group analysis within the UK.

In *The World Within the Group* (2014a) I argued that the original paradigm of group analysis has run its course. I laid down reasons for this and offered several new arenas of inquiry with the purpose of reinvigoration. Now a sixty-year-old (unlike the age of a person, how we date the birth of a discipline has some leeway) the current state of group analysis is in need of diagnosis. Granted that this may be more symptom than diagnosis, one contender is "discipline anxiety", resulting from our slow progress as a discipline, including our virtual absence in academic and popular life, and the risk of ever-reduced relevance within the wider field of psychotherapies; the word "crisis" could also be used. I will not address the issue of formal research, which would require far more space, but note its relative rarity and poor quality in our field, which leaves the discipline seriously exposed (for more on this, see the systematic review by Blackmore et al., 2010).

There are a number of possible responses to discipline anxiety, which are the subject of this chapter. To anticipate the argument in board terms, there is: (a) a risk at one end of the continuum of retreating into the comforts of a classicism, with endless repetition and reassertion of Foulkes and his basic assumptions; (b) anxious attempts to hitch our discipline to currently influential expressions (such as the term "relational", and the use of the qualifier "social" as a universal prefix, and so forth), as if these in themselves do anything other than reach out for a credibility we do not otherwise have. At the more positive end, (c) there is a need to develop newer, bolder scholarship and theoretical models (more pressingly, as noted, formal research; psychotherapy that lacks research withers), particularly around applied group-analytic approaches. There is no wish to debunk the entirety of group analysis, nor to devalue many innovations, but rather to address a trend of conservatism and complacency that has set in. I argue that we need to come down from "Magic Mountain" and all isolationist positions concerning our declining influence. Neither self-righteous indignation nor lyrical pleas help, and neither does it help if we fail to learn the symbolic message of Cnut (King Canute), that we cannot turn back the tide of inexorable events. Learning more actively and developing with, as distinct to hitching to, adjacent disciplines and therapies is, in my view, essential. We need to reposition ourselves as best we can and avoid a temptation to retreat. In this regard, and as a subcomponent of my case, I argue that group analysis has outlived its original dependence upon psychoanalysis, the parent discipline; worryingly, the former is likely tainted by some of the historical stance of superiority adopted by the latter, in many quarters. I am, on the other hand, reassured by many conversations with colleagues who also see the need for change and to adapt to the "real world".

Group retreats

I propose to talk in term of "group retreats" and "group enclaves" as an alternative to the "psychic retreats" of John Steiner.[1] The latter are described in terms of a kind of psychic geography, as places in(to) which (always) disturbed individuals hide; in his words, "withdrawal to a refuge where the patient was relatively free from anxiety but where development was minimal" (Steiner, 1990, p. 14). O'Shaughnessy's (1992) "Enclaves and excursions" uses a similar notion, as illustrated by examples from stunted analyses where "real contact" is avoided and the threat of change kept at bay. Unlike these notions, however, group retreats or group enclaves do not necessarily suggest disturbance (itself an enigmatic term, easy to use and hard to define), but rather indicate the way a group or organisation becomes preservative, and later complacent, once it fulfils its core function, such as delivering training, running courses, providing affiliation, and so forth. There is a novelty effect with disciplines, at the start, when practice is growing, training is established, trade journals are created, and so forth, but in times of challenge and reduced cultural hold, organisations can turn inwards to reassure themselves of their core identity and validity at the cost of remaining ignored and unseen elsewhere; in which case, renewal is replaced by repetition. Such organisations provide more shelter than development. Although he never offered an analysis of psychoanalytic institutes, Foulkes (1964, p. 121) uses the expressive term "cells", as well as "cultures", and "schools within the psychoanalytic movement". So what happens when cell growth is stunted?

In an incisive paper, Jungian analyst Jean Knox (2013) draws attention to the diminishing role played by psychoanalytic or psychodynamic therapies, at least in the public sector, but not entirely, arguing that training institutes risk becoming the equivalent of "psychic retreats" from the real world; again, I prefer the word group retreats on the grounds that these are organisations not persons. She suggests that initially trainees may seek a comforting, confirming alternative to the disappointments of the world outside by seeking training, with the like-minded, but that on qualification may face a second disappointment, this time in terms of declining opportunities to practice, although one should not generalise too much about the motivations and experiences of trainees. Using pragmatist philosophy, she demonstrates how institutes can develop a protective, siege mentality and defend their preferred theories on the basis of the inherited tenacity of their tradition and use of authorities. As is well known, different psychotherapy organisations and institutes seldom talk with each other, or engage with each other's traditions, and struggle with the question of how they reach out to the wider pubic, no doubt with varying success. In terms of their written traditions, psychotherapy can and often does suffer from a narrowness of citation and dependence on preferred theories and the authors associated with them. Roustang (1982) traces the inherent institutional binds that result from long processes of analytic discipleship and transmission—each with their venerated founders, lines of descent, loyalty, and isolation—splendid or otherwise—that accompanies it. In his observant comparison of analytic institutes with "secret societies" (the latter being the subject of a classic essay by Georg Simmel, whom the author quotes), Rustin (1991, p. 101) comments on the persistence of a certain type of self-image, of a "small enclave of moral and mutual enlightenment in an indifferent or hostile world". Organisations may aspire to be Janus-faced, but as often as not tend to turn inwards, talking a form of private language.

At a cultural level, it is interesting to speculate on the lack of hold of group analysis—unlike psychoanalysis (itself in decline, outside the academic field). As for the latter, despite its marginality as a public form of therapy, it elicited considerable cultural interest from the start—including in the form of hostility but never indifference; indeed, it had an electrifying effect. It is not difficult to see why, as Freud's excavations of the "dark half" of our natures was revolutionary at the time and aesthetically attractive (Ellenberger, 1970; Woolf, 1981). It found ready carriage within culture, and this largely because of its multivalent quality (Hinshelwood, 1995). This cultural "take up" remains the case in many areas, occasionally boosted by essayists and popular writers such as Christopher Bollas, Adam Phillips, and Stephen Grosz. Group analysis has no equivalent cultural resonance and is rarely named in discourses and disciplines away from it, and, more worrying still, by those nearby, such as social psychology. Why?

First, let us touch further upon the contrast with psychoanalysis. As Foucault (1977) proposes, Freud was a "founder of discursivity"; he created a vast vocabulary of human, unconscious life that is permanently associated with him. Some would say that his influence was simply a result of his being an outstanding writer, with a grand and incomparable style (Bloom, 1973). We saw in the preceding chapter how Freud's explorations of the new domain of the psychological interior was bound up with and contributed to a confessional culture and modernity.

Foulkes and group analysis has no comparable presence, for rather obvious reasons, given that by the time of his breakthrough the modern therapeutic culture of the self was already well in place, indeed was saturated by many strands of its practice. Arguably, the names he brought, those various "group analytic factors" and emphasis on communication, failed to stand out in a significant manner. Even the notion of "matrix" was prefigured in other, adjacent ideas, of which I would suggest Lewin's (1951) field theory is a notable example (Lewin also coined the term "group dynamics"). Further, there is no equivalent of the foundational essay, in the way in which Freud's (1921c) *Group psychology and the Analysis of the Ego* was, and no major contributions to a wider theory of culture. Group analysis has not inspired a novel, film, or leading cultural theory, and, in many group-work textbooks, is absent or barely mentioned. Could the reasons be mundane, such as the unexceptional quality and limited scope of Foulkes' writing? And Foulkes died before writing his book of "big theory", as was promised. Or is it to do with the fact that his was no longer the era of grand psychological discovery? To use a spatial metaphor, the territory into which he came was already cultivated and any new therapy, like group analysis, struggled to mark its place on the map. There were, however, ambitious and critical moments where an embryonic group analysis did gain traction, such as in the cradle of World War Two psychiatry, through the use of what Foulkes innocuously called "talking groups" at Northfield Military Hospital, and the subsequent birth (of course, there were precursors before this time) of therapeutic communities. Even with the latter, however, a pioneer such as Tom Main, director of the Cassel Hospital, who gave the first S. H. Foulkes Memorial Lecture (1981), refers only nominally to anything that might be considered specific to group analysis; as if wishing to make his own mark, and to own a brand, he says in his lecture on the concept of the therapeutic community, "while this lecture is offered to the memory of Michael Foulkes it is not primarily about him" (Main, 1989, p. 123). The other therapeutic community pioneer, Maxwell Jones, of the Henderson Hospital, was even less influenced by the analytic world (neither group analysis nor psychoanalysis) and took his cues from work therapy and psychodrama, and within the paradigm of social psychiatry (Jones, 1958).

With the creation of the "small group" convening for therapy, at first private, then in the health service, group analysis had its coming out (Foulkes, E., 1998). In sketching developments in psychotherapy during the 1960s, Foulkes (1964) notes the profusion of some new, quite active group approaches. Meanwhile, with the expansion of out-patient therapies, the 1970s was dubbed by Rosenbaum (writing an introduction to a mid-seventies edition of Foulkes, 1957), the "decade of the group" (Rosenbaum, 1975, p. xi). Arguably, by that time, Foulksean ideas were diffuse enough to be absorbed by other group approaches. Why this absorption? To understand this, we need to look back yet earlier, one might say to the non-clinical era of "the group" and its social conditions of emergence.

The psychological complex

In one of his successive contributions to understanding the contemporary "psychological complex", Rose (1990) traces the many ways in which new productions and regulations of subjectivity have come about. Within an increasingly variegated matrix of therapies, he argues that the war and post-war context "gave rise to new ways of construing institutional life in terms of 'human relations' and 'the group'" (p. 15). With this arose new forms of expertise, of therapeutic authority, and a desire to maximise human resources in institutional life, nowhere so important as in industry. This in turn links to wider development in liberal democracy, the art of governing "from a distance", and the requirement that modern citizens be regulators of themselves. The government of morale and related promotion of productivity were seen as critical. Rose (op. cit., p. 214) observes that "[t]he vocabularies of the therapeutic are increasingly deployed in every practice addressed to human problems". Given this proliferation of concerns and emergent sources of expertise, including the building of distinct professions, by the 1960s and 1970s group analysis was but a tiny part of a much larger complex, wherein lies its low visibility. "The group" had already, before Foulkes, been opened as a fertile field of thought, argument, and administration, not so much in the arena of personal therapy, but in the social spaces of the factory, hospital, schoolroom, and office (Rose, 1992). So too, interestingly, was there an emphasis on "communication", which was already seen as a vital aid to the improving functioning of groups and to the resolution of potential problems.

The risk of retreat remains, nowadays. The pioneers have largely gone, and many after them also, creating transmission anxiety. I have argued that our relative lack of research, historical low visibility, and lack of cultural "up-take" are serious issues. This is true even in areas where we like to claim that we have the edge over other analytic approaches, such as in our claims to have a "social" view of unconscious life. Space prevents me from addressing the wider area of group-analytic theory of the social unconscious or of large group phenomena. The fact remains that few outside our discipline and symposia quote us. Decline of the discipline is a concern and, in the light of apparent "loss of ground", I hear some continuing to assert complacent sentiments such as "But we know it works" and sounding warnings against any "surrender" of our principles.

Paradigms: conservatism, tension, change

The work of Thomas Kuhn on the philosophy of science created a stir in its time. I will leave aside the broader question: Is group analysis a science, or some other form of practice and inquiry?.[2] Suffice to say that Foulkes (1947) in optimistic, post-war flourish, talks of group analysis as "a new science in which psychology and sociology meet". Later, Foulkes and Anthony (1957, p. 269) address a dynamic, even if not a precise "science of psychotherapy", and looks to a time in which psychotherapy "becomes a social science" (Foulkes, 1969b, p. 206). I shall use the word "science" loosely, however, as constituting a rigorous form of inquiry that informs, tests, and in principle constrains the formation of explanatory concepts.

Kuhn's (1962) most famous idea is that of paradigm, by which he means a particular way of seeing the world and articulating a given field of problems or puzzles. Challenging the serial, cumulative notion of steady progress in science, Kuhn instead saw its many discontinuities. "Normal" phases of science, a kind of period of confident business-as-usual, contrasts with "revolutionary" phases in which disciplines experience crisis and uncertainty. "Normal science does not aim at novelty but at clearing up the status quo. It tends to discover what it expects to discover," says Hacking (2012). In other words, a shared framework, called either paradigm or disciplinary matrix (another of Kuhn's useful phrases), becomes disrupted when anomalies cannot be reconciled, when there are articulations of discontent, divisions, and debates over fundamentals. A crisis may eventually result in a revolutionary change in world-view that constitutes a paradigm shift, although succession is not without its attendant anxiety (Britton, 1998).

In one of his essay collections, Kuhn (1977) observes that if investigations break with a tradition they may give rise to a new one, in a dynamism that he speaks of in terms of the "essential tension" of scientific research. He argues that the original scientist (again, let us follow his image of scientist for the time being) is someone rooted in tradition but who also discovers "new rules" and "new pieces" of the puzzle (op. cit., p. 237), is both a traditionalist and an innovator. That picture could apply to Foulkes, so that we have the Foulkes deeply rooted in psychoanalytic tradition, and the Foulkes who constructs the "hybrid"[3] that is group analysis, which draws upon and borrows from a much wider field, including neurology (at least at the level of analogy), gestalt theory (again, as a metaphor), acknowledges the social psychology of Kurt Lewin, war-time psychiatry, and others.

One of the features of Kuhn's theory is that is gives scope for, and choice over, a variety of theories in any given disciplinary matrix. For the psychotherapies, however, this contains a risk and an opportunity. On the risk side, psychotherapy journals are sometimes criticised for giving the impression that clinicians can write and claim what they like, as there are no obvious "tests" or independent process of validation; their authors self-authorise when they write about "what is going on", in "the transference" , "the group", and so on. Borch-Jacobsen and Shamdasani (2012) argue this tendency goes back a long way, back in fact to Freud's immunising of psychoanalysis at different levels, which effectively excluded it from "the overt, public, critical context of normal science" (p. 23). Knox (2013) likewise notes the baleful effects of previous psychoanalytic arrogance, including hostility towards research. It will be a tragedy if group analysis fails to learn the lessons of this.

Beyond Foulkes: the road less travelled by ... .?

On the positive side of course, disciplines are strengthened by an openness to a variety of influences and research, and require continual growth. The essayist, Waldo Emerson (1841, p. 44) remarked of institutions, that they are "the lengthened shadow of one man". The sexist inference aside, one can ask the question of whether Foulkes has got in the way of group analysis. Dalal (1998) addresses a movement, the equivalent of a paradigm shift perhaps, sub-entitled, "towards a post-Foulksean group analysis". He locates the potential for this in the work of Norbert Elias in particular. Whist I find myself largely in agreement with this, for all his talk of a "radical" contrasting with an "orthodox" Foulkes, I do not find his proposals radical enough, for two main reasons. The first concerns invoking the figure of Elias, undoubtedly an outstanding social scientist, who created the historical sociology that views human subjects as the product of "figurations", networks of interdependence that are structured yet constantly subject to change. My concern is that group analysts have seldom done much with Elias beyond citing him, and rarely pursued new historical research of , for example, the type illustrated by Nikolas Rose, cited above, who amongst other endeavours has tried to situate the invention of "the group" within a wide field of "psy sciences" and related social conjunctures. An exception is the work of Malcolm Pines, although his historical reflections are principally confined to psychoanalysis, group analysis, and psychodynamic traditions of the twentieth century. There are many relevant strands in historical research, before and since Elias, upon which group analysts could draw. In short, I suggest that the name of "Elias" needs to be more than the discipline's symbolic figurehead; his major contribution does not exempt us from developing new, imaginative, long-term perspectives on human beings. As Liston (2012) puts it, "history is not just 'background' but rather the very stuff out of which can be constructed a proper understanding of the human condition as we observe it today. Developments in many disciplines are pointing in the same intellectual direction, that is, away from a retreat into the present and towards the need for a longer-term perspective." Two brief examples. The first is that of "history from below", to which I have made brief reference in other chapters, as it draws attention to the many excluded and occluded figures of the past (and present) who, moreover, were often treated as people without a history (Hobsbawm, 1997). A second example are the historical researches of Foucault, a curiously neglected figure in group analysis, given that his concerns are arguably more relevant and proximal for us than those of Elias (although both share a similar conception of power; Burke, 2012).

The second set of reasons relate to a number of frankly repetitive publications within group analysis concerning the social and relational nature of human beings. There are many instances of this, which I cannot help but think reflect discipline anxiety and the desire to possess respectable credentials; indeed, they are fast becoming part of our self-reassuring imaginary. Taking Dalal (1998, 2001) again as but one example, his numerous discussions of the social and individual, of the primacy of either, and related philosophical dualities, have an exhausted feel, and however "right" their deconstruction is, they do not in themselves enable new work to be done. The pragmatists were right long ago, that we should not be detained by sterile dualisms and other unproductive habits of thinking. A final point on this is that much of what group analysts say about our being as "social, through and through", and the "social nature of persons" (e.g., Ormay, 2012, Stacey, 2001), and related emphasis on "the relational", seems to have arrived late in the day and one wonders what is being emphasised by such insistences? Such words risk becoming simply codes, badges of respectability.

For all our rhetorical flourish and self-reassurance, most of what we emphasise has been said decades before—one has only to think of Georg Simmel's (1971) science of "sociality and reciprocal effects", John Dewey's (1958) pragmatism, or the "primary inter-subjectivity" as developed by Husserl and the phenomenologists. Then again, many of the broadly social constructionist perspectives that we now adopt were formulated by sociologists since the 1960s, of which Berger and Luckmann's (1966) text is a classic example. As for an encapsulation of "social mind", an idea attractive to group analysts, what finer statement could there be than that of sociologist Cooley (1907, p. 675), who wrote, "Mind is an organic whole made up of co-operating individualities, in somewhat the same way that the music of an orchestra is made up of divergent but related sounds. No one would think it necessary or reasonable to divide the music into two kinds—that made by the whole and that of particular instruments; and no more are there two kinds of mind—the social mind and the individual mind."

Parental relations: does group analysis defer to psychoanalysis?

Foulkes saw no opposition between psychoanalysis and group analysis, and remained a practising psychoanalyst throughout his life. In his discussion of the pair, a theme that circulates throughout his writings, Foulkes is caught in a play of tension in which languages of deviation and creative innovation are both present. It is as if he is forever trying to find himself in the thick of such tensions, and opts for the diplomatic formulation.

In his first book, he writes, "[t]he present writers stand firmly on the grounds of classical psychoanalysis ... ." (Foulkes & Anthony, 1957, p. 16), and is dismissive of "deviations" from Freud, which are labelled "neo-Freudian" or "neo-analytic". In the same work, he pays tribute to the method in Freud's *The Interpretation of Dreams*, as "our Bible" (op. cit., p. 38), with no hint of irony. This relates to his belief in the operations of the unconscious, use of the method of free (group) association, and the privileging of dreams in the clinical material. With a nod to the unconscious, he refers to the importance of the group analyst as "expert at translation" (op. cit., p. 245). Later, Foulkes underscores the importance of thorough acquaintance with Freud's structural mode of personality and his approach to dreams, defences, and so forth (Foulkes & Anthony, 1957). The interpretation of the dream is again presented as *via regia* ("royal road") to the unconscious.

At the same time, from the beginning, Foulkes asserts his right to develop group analysis. Rejecting any idea of absolute truths, he argues that group therapy not be limited by present-day psychoanalytic concepts: "group-analysis is free to develop within the large framework of psychotherapy" (Foulkes & Anthony, 1957, p. 17). Later, his tone is yet more confident: "it was an act of liberation to work in what I consider a new field, group analysis, where one could build anew without in the least losing one's psychoanalytic foundation" (Foulkes, 1975, p. 287). And in a revealing passage about Freud's work as being, "like a great work of art" (op. cit.), any reference to a symbolic Bible is gone. In *Therapeutic Group Analysis* (1964) there is a series of papers on the relationship group analysis/psychoanalysis. In one he warns of a "Monroe Doctrine" (i.e., an imperial, "go it alone" stance) whereby psychoanalysis might attempt to exist "unhampered" by developments in other fields. "Meanwhile," he pointedly observes, "other disciplines have not been standing still" (op. cit., p. 142).

Finally, in a late paper, possibly part of a promised book on theory (Malcolm Pines, personal communication), Foulkes (2003, p. 316), whilst expressing "complete adherence" to and "lifelong preoccupation" with psychoanalysis, uses the term "post-psychoanalysis" and refers to the "need to get beyond the metaphysics of psychoanalysis". The paper is all too brief, tantalisingly, with no elaboration of what this could mean.

Issues and suggestions

In *The World Within the Group* (2014a), I explored ideas which might provide valuable resources for group analysts, drawn from the realms of modern social theory and history. In this book I offer more, including the theory of rhetoric, positioning theory, and the paradigm of the dialogical self, all of which help us to see communication between people in a complex light and the "self" as performative process and as multi-storied. Whatever we draw upon, the basis for paradigm shifts needs to be inter- (or trans-) disciplinary, and, I argue, broadly psychosocial in nature, rather than mainly psychoanalytic. I believe it long overdue to better insert into our field the (modern) psychology and sociology that Foulkes himself saw during his time as being of critical relevance.

Although the following points are highly schematic and condensed, they outline some of the concerns and challenges that I have in mind:

- Regarding an academic hold for group analysis, Pines (2006) posed the question, "How can group analysis become an academic discipline?", addressing both the demands for enhanced clinical training and academic contribution or viability. His conclusion is optimistic, mine less so. Sadly, as noted, we are absent even in those disciplines that are our potential closest neighbours, such as social psychology and sociology.
- As a theory, group analysis was established with the help of metaphors and analogies from other areas, such as neurology, gestalt theory, figurational sociology, and the like. Arguably, however, these are "weak" analogies, undeveloped from the start and, certainly nowadays, no longer serve us.
- Group analysis developed in dependence upon psychoanalysis. As has been explored, this was an unequal relationship and our sources need to be far wider, and more empirical. Further, that earlier tradition, exemplified by Foulkes, of the double-qualified psychoanalyst and group analyst has effectively gone. Still, throughout its history, Carter (2002, p. 132), points out how group analysis has a tendency "to look back to its mother (psychoanalysis) for security". Perhaps there was always—and might still be—a degree of "psychoanalysis envy" embedded in group-analytic culture.
- The domain of the "psychosocial" offers a more fertile field than of psychoanalysis per se, although in this transitional field, too, there are differences regarding the centrality, or otherwise, that should accord to psychoanalysis (Frosh, 2014). Further, as regards psychoanalysis, "empirical psychoanalysis" has done a great deal to renew that field and rescue it from much of the speculation and mystique of old (Fonagy, 1996, 2003). Historically, psychoanalysis (and group analysis) was defined as an approach characterised by "freedom

from constraint and counted treatment length not in terms of number of sessions but in terms of years" (Fonagy, 2003, p. 73), in marked contrast to an era of empirically validated treatments and brief structured interventions.

- The "pioneer generation", and many after, has largely disappeared, or are no longer active, which creates questions of transmission. Who develops, or, putting it more objectively, how is the discipline to develop, and in which directions?

- Related to the above, and as Knox (2013) also argues, we cannot rely on the use of "authority" as an instrument of reassurance and validation. I recall my surprise when, attending the general course in group analysis in the late 1990s, just how little evidence was cited as compared to the authority of clinical examples and quotation of well-known group analysts. To put it bluntly, "eminence-based practice" has to give way to "evidence-based practice". We cannot maroon ourselves and discount the rise of contemporary clinical guidance and modern norms of clinical governance.

- Many of the sites in which slow-open, exploratory, and heterogeneous group analysis in the UK was developed or had influence have receded or disappeared altogether, including an older era of day centres, a range of therapeutic communities, and most public sector psychotherapy departments. This means a dramatic decline in our institutional relevance.

- Clinical practice is not a sealed laboratory that replaces the need for other kinds of evaluation and test. All too often, if we only rely on our observations, we create conveniently smoothed narratives of what we offer (Spence, 1982) in reported accounts of group life. And the clinical group has to be supplemented by study of the empirical group. In this regard, Nitsun's (2015) call for a more "real world" group analysis, in its modified forms and applications, is an important one.

- Infant observations are a requirement for many psychoanalytic trainings, and group analytic trainings require an equivalent. One clear candidate would be that of formalised group observations, of nonclinical situations, where the observer has no other role to play than as observer. This would build a wider base of evidence and appreciation of group process and dynamics.

- To be consistent with recovery-based practice, it would be important to have not only more clinical audits but also client-centred (indeed, client- involved) research, such as the use of IPA, to see how members of groups *actually* see and experience groups, rather than how we prefer to interpret those experiences. The absence of service-user perspective was highlighted in the systematic review (Blackmore et al., 2010). Although this is anecdotal, and thus suffers from the same complaint I am aiming at others, I frequently hear clients in groups (outside of training contexts) emphasising the "supportive" aspect more than any "analytic" aspects, and this would be interesting to research formally; the supportive aspects, however, may appear less exciting to write about.

- There is, at the same time, a burgeoning of group-analytic literature, of which "The New International Library of Group Analysis" (Karnac) is a leading example. However, this alone may not be sufficient to increase our relevance, either at the level of theory or of practice.

- We need to reconnect with developments in social psychology, several examples of which I have used in this book. We also need to take better account of modern perspectives on the cognitive, some would call it the "new", unconscious, in addition to the dynamic unconscious—a perspective that includes many group-relevant phenomena as automatic processes, working-memory, language processing, impression formation, self-regulation, and many others (Hassin, Uleman & Bargh, 2005).

- I know many colleagues who, like me, are all too aware of our marginal position. Many agree that how we communicate what we do needs to change, to become more accessible.

- We live in a social and therapeutic world that is vastly different to how it was constituted in the hey-day of group analysis. Part of this modern world relates to a more informed public, and the requirement for more democratic access to knowledge. We can ill afford to retreat behind technical terms and whatever private language we have established.

- Not only this, but, in Nitsun's (2015, p. 108) words, "[i]n the end our survival may depend on reducing the narcissism of differences, and fostering sufficient openness and humility to embrace difference." This means developing ideas that speak well, ideas that have reach, travel, and accessibility. To have wider foundations and broader appeal is an ambitious but also a humble project, and involves a preparedness to overcome a narcissism associated with "sharing space", including disciplinary space (Nitsun, personal communication; Britton, 2003).

Conclusion

Paradigm change constitutes a threat to previous theory and practice, but is necessary at certain junctures for growth to occur. It signifies a transition, but, like a ship changing course, its longer-term consequences cannot be predicted. Disciplines in crisis can also retreat, as can the institutions associated with them, so as to reassure themselves of the validity of existing knowledge and practice—the equivalent of the "Monroe doctrine" that Foulkes gave warning of in relation to psychoanalysis. All approaches need a degree of self-reassurance, but we have to be careful of our claims; Pines (1998) points out that "[p]sychoanalytic institutes, like many communities, consolidate themselves around mythologies" (p. 127). We need to learn from our own knowledge of group process, that disciplines and organisations can, like individuals, stop developing and ossify.

Notes

1. I am claiming no originality for the term group retreats, which is used in slightly different ways by authors such as Hopper (1991) and Mojović (2011). As far as I understand their work, such retreats are likely associated with social trauma (including so-called "traumatised societies", although both raise the possibility of more positive retreats), and are conceptualised mainly with reference to psychoanalytic theory and the isolation and sealing-off of unacceptable experiences, annihilation anxiety, and so forth. My usage here is not specifically linked to trauma and is not tethered to psychoanalytic explanations as applied to groups; in this sense it is a more empirical, sociological notion.
2. Maraki's (2008) account suggests that the notion of different "discursive communities" might be more apposite to the field of therapy than that of scientific paradigms; different schools of psychoanalysis, he argues, vary to the degree to which they accept or encourage interpretive variance and autonomy. Related to the latter, one of the preferred self-images of group analysis is that it is more "open" as a therapy, is theoretically diverse, and accords prominence/priority to the "social".
3. In an interesting passage, Foulkes (1961, p. 148) poses the question that if his group analytic approach shares some common ground with non-analytic approaches (he mentions Moreno and Lewin), then does that make it a "hybrid formation"? Although he answers in the negative, implying that a hybrid is an undesirable state of compromise (he quotes Freud's term, pertaining to symptoms, "compromise formation"),

he suggests that engagement with common ground is an important venture, a "dynamic proposition" (op. cit.). This may be a semantic point, but I see no problem with the language of the hybrid, influenced as it is both by hard sciences (botany, biology) and the social—with its contemporary connotations of cultural blending, partial identities, multiple selves, and so forth.

EPILOGUE

"Where shall we start?" is the sort of comment I might well make when first seeing a client, a way of opening that does not confine the dialogue to any particular region or preconceived expectation (e.g., "my past", "the problem", "symptoms", "reason for coming"), any, and more of which, can be explored as the meeting unfolds. Beginning this way is an invitation to open speech-permission to narrate, if one wills. Not only this, but my use of the "we" pronoun (as distinct from, e.g., "Where do *you* want to start from?") acknowledges the mutuality of psycho-therapy as an endeavour and that in speaking, someone else is always there to be addressed. Mutuality does not mean that the "I"s disappear. Whatever follows from this point onwards—be it a pause, an anxious confession, watering of the eyes, a composed description, discomposed distress, a question, and so forth—*is* the formation of a meaningful con-nection. From that connection and narrative contact, agreement to a fur-ther meeting, or to therapy, arises; and even if we only see that person once, for whatever reason, we still hope that the meeting will have pro-vided good food for thought.

This book is concerned with the intimacies of speech, acts of expres-sion, voice, description and narrative space—in how our very lives "speak". In using "permission to narrate" as my summary term for the activity of psychotherapy, I suggest that clients can find themselves in and through what they say, and how they say it. Older and existing narratives are elucidated and, through exploration, are revised. New inflections appear and, in time, may be a different sort of voice. A retelling, from a new position. A counter-narrative perhaps. Personal paradigm change. And a different outcome ... there are all sorts of possibilities. None of this means that I privilege the verbal, the left brain, or talk, in and of itself. Indeed, there is a risk that in narrating all, something is lost. Narrative might absorb too much of an experience and the usual conventions of telling and narrative ordering may prove unhelpful to a given individual. What resists narrative coherence is itself of interest and value, as is the silence that comes to rest between the many episodes of what is said. Silence is an altogether different sound.

There is a personal connection with all this of course, granting myself permission to narrate, including the act of writing this book. "You don't write because you want to say something, you write because you have something to say," remarked F. Scott Fitzgerald. It is a subtle, but important distinction. Having something to say takes a long while to ferment, and involves a growing-up or growing-out. There are two sorts of growing up for me—first, overcoming a long-term (and thankfully largely overcome) tendency to reticence and lack of confidence in my authority, compensated for, no doubt, in various ways along the years. That, I believe, was in large measure reflective of a family/cultural set of narratives about not "showing off", not "showing yourself up", "keeping it quiet", not "making a fuss", and never "washing your dirty linen in public"—or even for that matter in private. And soundproof your home as much as you can against the disturbances of the world outside. Then there is the professional growing up and no longer living under the apprenticeship, dependence, and shadow of others—other writers, admired figures, hallowed traditions. And yet, from all these sources, this forest of inspirations, I am able to find my voice. A friend said of me that I am a different sort of psychologist, and a dissident sort of psychotherapist. Likely so. Having something to say.

So, where shall we finish? Where to bring down the full stop? How about with these words from a fine song by Jackson Browne:

> Stand in the open;
> The next voice you hear will be your own.

GLOSSARY

The following glossary does not repeat any of the terms defined in the glossary of my previous work (Weegmann, 2014a), but is complementary to it, and, similarly, has a transdisciplinary emphasis.

Counternarrative

In relation to the theory of narrative and narration (see under "narrative"), counternarratives arise as alternative accounts that, usually, question existing and dominant narratives, whether in the family, in groups, or within the individual's own internalised life experiences. Counternarratives help a person to effectively "re-write" and "re-author" (see below) their story.

Dialogical psychology

A research and psychotherapy practice paradigm as developed by Hubert Hermans and others, that unites certain psychologies of the self (James, Mead) and Bakhtin's dialogical approach to literature.

Discipline anxiety

Discipline anxiety refers to those preoccupations that can mark a particular discipline or field of inquiry, and which are a defensive response to new challenges, lack of sufficient evidence, anomalies, and so forth.

Fascination

A captivating form of attention shown to another person, idea, movement, and so forth. Fascination may have both a "soft", undefined quality (such as an inspiring walk in nature), or may be characterised by exclusivity or fixation, with the dismissal and downgrading of alternatives.

Group retreats

A metaphorical notion, group or organisational retreats function like sanctuaries or places of safety from the pressures and demands of the outside world. Although group retreats offer a measure of protection, their disadvantage is that they reduce adaptation to change and to new requirements. As such, they may inhibit growth.

Monsters

Monsters, beasts, demons, and other imaginary beings, play complex roles in society. In etymology, the monster "shows", "reveals", and "warns", although how such messages are read is the subject of many interpretations. Monsters are considered here in terms of what they might show us about the nature of human society and its preferred identity and self-definition at a group level.

Narratives

At its most general, narratives are the way in which we order and grasp experiences together into a meaningful whole; in a profound way, we are "story-telling animals" (MacIntyre). This book has considered the rhetorical aspects of narrative and those narratives of recovery that help people with mental distress and disorders to refigure and rebuild their lives.

Paradigm

Made famous by Thomas Kuhn, a paradigm is a set of concepts and principles that characterises a discipline at a given time. Paradigms provide model problems and practices for a given community of inquirers. A paradigm shift occurs when there is a significant break and reorganisation of the disciplinary field.

Permission to narrate

I use this expression (from Edward Said) as an emblem for psychotherapy, which invites clients to start telling us the story of themselves, to voice their concerns and the ways in which they are hampered. Progress in psychotherapy involves narrative change and a "re-authoring" (below) of experience.

Positioning

In everyday use, position is a spatial metaphor to do with placing, setting out, or situating. In the social theory that is used in this book, positioning concerns the ways in which we use words (and other discourses) to locate ourselves and others, including assumed rights, duties, and a variety of ascriptions.

Re-authoring

In narrative therapy, re-authoring concerns the emergence of a better founded, more integrated way of talking about and relating to one's experiences. The position of the speaking subject to their life changes, as from, for example, "underdog" to "equal", or "silly, frightened girl" to "confident, accomplished women", etc.

Recovery

Recovery refers to the ways in which people overcome psychosocial adversity and disorder, together with the values and narratives that sustain them. Narratives of recovery are particularly important to those who have faced major biographical disruption or set-back.

Revolution

Revolution can signify abrupt political change, significant social change (including a "slow revolution"), or change in attitudes, all of which carry high hopes and deep fears. As adjective, revolutionary change entails the complete overall of something and its replacement by a radical alternative.

Rhetoric

Classically, rhetoric was the art of effective speech (or writing) and persuasion—"winning the soul by discourse", according to Plato. Modern rhetoric theory is concerned with a much wider view of language, how we act upon other and are acted upon ourselves.

Speech act

In philosophy and linguistics, speech acts are utterances which have a key performative function, such as an apology, promise, request, command, refusal. These are "acts" in so far as a symbolic/actual action takes place; in speech act theory, language does much more than describe reality.

Voice

Although voice is literally the vocalised form that human communication takes, it is used metaphorically to describe the position and wider expression taken by the person. This could include aspects of tone, trajectory, force, legitimacy, authority, power, and so forth. In line with narrative theory, people might be said to be "many voiced", with competing or contradictory voices, past voice versus present, dominant versus submerged, conscious versus automatic, etc.

REFERENCES

Althusser, L. (1971). Freud and Lacan. In: *Lenin and Philosophy and Other Essays*. London: New Left.

Anderson, P. (1974). France. In: *Lineages of the Absolutist State*, Chapter Four). London: New Left.

Ara Krummel, M. (2011). *Crafting Jewishness in Medieval England: Legally Absent, Virtually Present*. New York: Palgrave Macmillan.

Arnold, M. (1888). *Civilization in the United States: First and Last Impressions*. Carlisle, MA: Applewood Books, 2007.

Aristotle (1997) *Poetics*. New York: Dover.

Aristotle (2004) *Rhetoric*. New York: Dover.

Auestad, L. (Ed.) (2014). *Nationalism and the Body Politic: Psychoanalysis and the Rise of Ethnocentrism and Xenophobia*. London, Karnac.

Augoustinos, M., & Tileaga, C. (2012). Editorial: Twenty-five years of discursive psychology. *British Journal of Social Psychology, 51*: 405–412.

Austin, J. L. (1962). *How to Do Things with Words*. Cambridge, MA: Harvard University Press.

Bale, A. (2006). *The Jew in the Medieval Book: English Antisemitisms, 1350–1500*. Cambridge: Cambridge University Press.

Bale, A. (2010). *Feeling Persecuted: Christians, Jews and Images of Violence in the Middle Ages*. London: Reaktion.

Ballesteros Gonzalez, A. (1996). "Deformed, unfinished, sent before my time". Monstrosity in *Richard III* and Mary Shelley's *Frankenstein*. *Sederi*, 7: 243–247.

Barnum, P. (2012). The monstrous Caribbean. In: A. Mittman & P. Dendle (Eds.), *The Ashgate Research Companion to Monsters and the Monstrous*. Farnham: Ashgate.

Barrows, S. (1981). *Distorting Mirrors: Visions of the Crowd in Late Nineteenth-century France*. New Haven: Yale University Press.

Behr, H. (2015). *The French Revolution: A Tale of Terror and Hope for our Times*. Eastbourne: Sussex Academic Press.

Berger, P., & Luckmann, T. (1966). *The Social Construction of Reality*. London: Penguin.

Biernacki, P. (1986). *Pathways from Heroin Addiction Recovery without Treatment*. Philadelphia, PA: Temple University Press.

Bildhauer, B. (2003). Blood, Jews and monsters in medieval culture. In: B. Bildhauer & R. Mills (Eds.), *The Monstrous Middles Ages*. Cardiff: University of Wales Press.

Bill, W. (1944). *Three Talks to Medical Societies*. New York: Alcoholics Anonymous World Services.

Bill, W. (1967). *As Bill Sees It: The AA Way of Life … Selected Writings of the AA's Co-Founder*. New York: Alcoholics Anonymous World Services.

Blackmore, C., Tantum, D., Parry, G. & Chambers, E. (2010). Report on a systematic review of the efficacy and clinical effectiveness of group analysis and analytic/dynamic group psychotherapy. *Group Analysis, 45/1*: 46–69.

Bloom, H. (1973). *The Anxiety of Influence: A Theory of Poetry*. New York: OUP.

Bogdan, R. (1988). *Freak Show: Presenting Human Oddities for Amusement and Profit*. Chicago: University of Chicago Press.

Borch, C. (2012). *The Politics of Crowds: An Alternative History of Sociology*. Cambridge: Cambridge University Press.

Borch-Jacobsen, M., & Shamdasani, S. (2008). Interprefactions: Freud's legendary science. *History of the Human Sciences, 21*: 1–25.

Borch-Jacobsen, M., & Shamdasani, S. (2012). *The Freud Files: An Inquiry into the History of Psychoanalysis*. Cambridge: Cambridge University Press.

Borman, T. (2014). *Witches: James I and the English Witch Hunts*. London: Vintage.

Botting, F. (Ed.) (1991). *Making Monstrous: Frankenstein, Criticism, Theory*. Manchester: Manchester University Press.

Botting, F. (2014). *Gothic*. London: Routledge.

Boureau, A. (2006). *Satan and the Heretic: The Birth of Demonology in the Medieval West* (Trans. T. Fagan). Chicago: University of Chicago Press.

Bovey, A. (2002). *Monsters and Grotesques in Medieval Manuscripts*. London: The British Library.

Bradley, I. (2006). *The Call to Seriousness: The Evangelical Impact on the Victorians*. Oxford: Lion.

Brandell, G. (1979). *Freud: A Man of his Century*. Brighton: Harvester.

Briggs, A. (1985). The language of mass and masses in the 19th century. In: A. Briggs, *The Collected Essays of Asa Briggs* (Chapter Two). Hove: Harvester.

Briggs, A., & Burke, P. (2009). *A Social History of the Media: From Guttenberg to the Internet*. Cambridge: Polity.

Britton, R. (1998). *Belief and Imagination: Explorations in Psychoanalysis*. London: Routledge.

Britton, R. (2003). Narcissistic problems in sharing space. In: R. Britton, *Sex, Death and the Superego*. London: Karnac.

Brohan, E., Gauci, D., Sartorius, N., Thornicroft, G. (2010). Self-stigma, empowerment and perceived discrimination among people with bipolar disorder or depression in 13 European countries. *Journal of Affective Disorders, 129*: 56–63.

Burke, E. (1990). *Philosophical Enquiry into the Origins of Our Ideas of the Sublime and the Beautiful* (1757) (Ed. A. Phillips). Oxford: Oxford University Press.

Burke, E. (2006). *Reflections on the Revolution in France*. Mineola, NY: Dover.

Burke, K. (1969). *A Rhetoric of Motives*. Berkeley, CA: University of California Press.

Burke, K. (1998). Literature as equipment for living. In: D. H. Richter (Ed.), *The Critical Tradition: Classic Texts and Contemporary Trends*. Boston, MA: Bedford.

Burke, P. (1993). *The Art of Conversation*. Cambridge: Polity.

Burke, P. (2004). Frontiers of the monstrous. In: L. L. Knoppers & J. B. Landes (Eds.), *Monstrous Bodies/Political Monstrosities in Early Modern Europe* (Chapter One). Ithaca, NY: Cornell University Press.

Burke, P. (2012). Norbert Elias and the social history of knowledge. *Figurations, 1/1*. Online journal.

Burrows, S. (1981). *Distorting Mirrors: Visions of the Crowd in Late Nineteenth-century France*. New Haven, CT: Yale University Press.

Bury, M. (1982). Chronic illness as biographical disruption. *Sociology of Health and Illness, 4*: 167–182.

Butler, J. (1997). On linguistic vulnerability. In: *Excitable Speech: A Politics of the Performative* (pp. 1–41). New York: Routledge.

Bynum, C. W. (1995). *The Resurrection of the Body in Western Christianity: 200–1336*. New York: Columbia University Press.

Cantor, P. (1984). The nightmare of romantic idealism. In: P. Cantor, *Creature and Creator: Myth-Making and English Romanticism* (pp. 103–132). Cambridge: Cambridge University Press.

Carson, J., McManus, G., & Chander, A. (2010). Recovery: a selective review of the literature and resources. *Mental Health and Social Inclusion, 14*: 35–45.

Carter, D. (2002). Research and survive: a central question for group analysis. *Group Analysis, 35*: 119–134.

Caygill, H. (2013). *On Resistance: A Philosophy of Defiance*. London: Bloomsbury Academic.

Chaucer, G. (2005). *The Canterbury Tales* (Ed. J. Mann). London: Penguin.

Cohen, J. J. (Ed.) (1996). *Monster Theory*. Minneapolis, MN: University of Minnesota Press.

Cohen, J. J. (2012). Postscript: The promise of monsters. In: A. Mittman & P Dendle (Eds.), *The Ashgate Research Companion to Monsters and the Monstrous*. Farnham: Ashgate.

Cohn, N. (1967). *Warrant for Genocide: The Myth of the Jewish World-Conspiracy and the Protocols of the Elders of Zion*. New York: Harper & Row.

Cohn, N. (1975). *Europe's Inner Demons: The Demonization of Christians in Medieval Christendom*. London: Pimlico, 1993.

Collins, P. (2001). Quaker plaining as critical aesthetic. *Quaker Studies, 5*: 121–139.

Cook, J. W. (1996). Of men, missing links and nondescripts; the strange career of P. T. Barnum's "What is it?" exhibition. In: R. G. Thomson (Ed.), *Freakery: Cultural Spectacles of the Extraordinary Body*. New York: New York University Press.

Cooley, C. H. (1907). Social consciousness. *American Journal of Sociology, 12*: 675–694.

Cosin, B., Freeman, C., & Freeman, N. (1971). Critical empiricism criticised: the case of Freud. *Journal for the Theory of Social Behaviour, 1*: 122–151.

Cousins, M., & Hussain, A. (1984). *Michael Foucault*. London: Macmillan.

Cox, M., & Theilgaard, A. (1987). *Mutative Metaphors in Psychotherapy: the Aeolian Mode*. London: Tavistock.

Craton, L. (2009). *The Victorian Freak Show: The Significance of Disability and Physical Differences in 19th-Century Fiction*. Amherst, NY: Cambria.

Crawford, J. (2005). *Marvellous Protestantism: Monstrous Births in Post-Reformation England*. Baltimore, MD: John Hopkins University Press.

Crews, F. (2006). *Follies of the Wise: Dissenting Essays*. Emeryville, CA: Shoemaker Hoard.

Crockford, A. (2010). Distancing deformity: The case of Joseph Merrick. In: G. Spark, L. Findlay, P. MacPherson, & A. Wood (Eds.), *Alienation and Resistance: Representation in Text and Image* (Chapter Three). Newcastle upon Tyne: Cambridge Scholar's Press.

Dalal, F. (1998). *Taking the Group Seriously*. London: Jessica Kingsley.

Dalal, F. (2001). The social unconscious: a post-Foulksean perspective. *Group Analysis, 34*: 539–555.

Davies, B. (2000). *A Body of Writing, 1990–1999*. Walnut Creek, CA: AltaMira Press.

Davies, B., & Harré, R. (1999). Positioning and personhood. In: R. Harré & L. van Lagenhove (Eds.), *Positioning Theory: Moral Contexts of Intentional Action* (pp. 32–52). Malden, MA: Blackwell.

De Baecque, A. (1997). *The Body Politic. Corporeal Metaphor in Revolutionary France, 1770-1800* (Trans. C. Mandell). Stanford, CA: Stanford University Press.

Delany, S. (2002). Chaucer's prioress, the Jews and the Muslims. In: S. Delaney (Ed.), *Chaucer and the Jews: Sources, Contexts, Meanings* (Chapter 3). London: Routledge.

Derrida, J. (1988). An interview with Jacques Derrida (Trans. D. Alison). In: D. Wood & R. Bernasconi (Eds.), *Derrida and Difference*. Evanston, IL: Northwestern University Press.

Derrida, J. (1995). Passages—from traumatism to promise. In: E. Weber (Ed.), P. Kamuf (Trans.), *Points ...: Interviews, 1974–1994*. Palo Alto, CA: Stanford University Press.

Dewey, J. (1958). *Experience and Nature*. New York: Dover.

Dews, S., Kaplan, J., & Winner, E. (1995). Why not say it directly? The social functions of irony. *Discourse Processes, 19*: 347–367.

Dickens, C. (1844). *The Chimes: The Second Quarter*.

Dickens, C. (1859). *A Tale of Two Cities*.

Dodds, B. (2011). Bandit narratives in comparative perspective: Jaime el Barbudo and Robin Hood. *Social History, 36*: 465–481.

Douglas, M. (1970). *Natural Symbols*. London: Routledge.

Doyle, W. (2000). The execution of Louis XVI and the end of the French monarchy. *History Review, 36*: 21–25.

Durbach, N. (2010). *Spectacle of Deformity: Freak Shows and Modern British Culture*. Berkeley, CA: University of California Press.

Dwyer, (2015). "Citizen Emperor": Political power, popular sovereignty and the coronation of Napoleon I. *History, 100*: 40–57.

Eco, U. (2007). *On Ugliness*. New York: Rizzoli.

Edwards, D. (1999). Emotion discourse. *Culture and Psychology, 5*: 271–291.

Edwards, J., & Graulund, R. (2013). *Grotesque*. New York: Routledge.

Eisold, K. (1994). The intolerance of diversity in psychoanalytic institutions. *International Journal of Psychoanalysis, 75*: 785–800.

Elias, N. (1978). *The Civilising Process: The History of Manners*. Oxford: Blackwell.

Ellenberger, H. F. (1970). *The Discovery of the Unconscious: The History and Evolution of Dynamic Psychiatry*. New York: Basic.

Elliot, A. (2002). *Psychoanalytic Theory: An Introduction* (2nd Ed.). Basingstoke: Palgrave.

Elliott, J. H. (1970). *The Old World and the New: 1492–1650*. Cambridge: Cambridge University Press.

Emerson, R. W. (1841). Self-reliance. In: *Emerson's Essays* (pp. 31–66). New York: Harper & Row, 1981.

Emerson, R. W. (2007). *Journals of Ralph Waldo Emerson, with Annotations, 1841–1844*. Pittsburgh, PA: Carnegie Mellon University Press.

Erikson, E. (1963). *Childhood and Society* (2nd Ed.). New York: W. W. Norton.

Fahy, T. (2006). *Freak Shows and the Modern American Imagination*. New York: Palgrave Macmillan.

Fairclough, M. (2013). *The Romantic Crowd: Sympathy, Controversy and Print Culture*. Cambridge: Cambridge University Press.

Flores, P. (1988). *Group Psychotherapy with Addicted Populations*. New York: The Haworth Press.

Fonagy, P. (1996). The future of an empirical psychoanalysis. *British Journal of Psychotherapy, 13*: 106–118.

Fonagy, P. (2003). Psychoanalysis today. *World Psychiatry, 2*: 73–80.

Forrester, J. (1980). Michel Foucault and the history of psychoanalysis. *History of the Sciences, 18*: 287–303.

Forrester, J., & Appignanesi, L. (2001). *Freud's Women*. London: Weidenfeld & Nicolson.

Foucault, M. (1973). *The Birth of the Clinic: An Archaeology of Medical Perception*. New York: Pantheon.

Foucault, M. (1975). *Discipline and Punish: The Birth of the Prison*. London: Penguin.

Foucault, M. (1977). *Language, Counter- Memory, Practice: Selected Essays and Interviews* (Ed. and trans. D. F. Bouchard). Ithaca, NY: Cornell University Press.

Foucault, M. (1979). *The History of Sexuality, Volume 1*. London: Penguin.

Foulkes, E. (1998). Fifty years of group analysis. *Group Analysis, 31*: 437–446.

Foulkes, S. H. (1947). Group psychotherapy in the light of psychoanalysis. In: S. H. Foulkes, *Therapeutic Group Analysis* (Chapter Six). London: Karnac, 1984.

Foulkes, S. H. (1948). *Introduction to Group-Analytic Psychotherapy*. London: Karnac, 1983.

Foulkes, S. H. (1957). *Group Analytic Psychotherapy: Method and Principles*. London: Karnac, 1984.

Foulkes, S. H. (1961). The position of group analysis today, with special reference to the role of the Group-Analytic Society (London). In: S. H. Foulkes, *Selected Papers: Psychoanalysis and Group Analysis* (pp. 145–150). London: Karnac, 1990.

Foulkes, S. H. (1964). *Therapeutic Group Analysis*. London: Karnac, 1984.

Foulkes, S. H. (1966). Some basic concepts in group psychotherapy. In: S. H. Foulkes, *Selected Papers: Psychoanalysis and Group Analysis* (pp. 151–158). London: Karnac, 1990.

Foulkes, S. H. (1969a). "Recollections of my visit to Freud". In: S. H. Foulkes, *Selected Papers: Psychoanalysis and Group Analysis* (pp. 21–28). London: Karnac, 1990.

Foulkes, S. H. (1969b). Two opposed views of social psychiatry: the issue. In: S. H. Foulkes, *Selected Papers: Psychoanalysis and Group Analysis* (pp. 195–207). London: Karnac, 1990.

Foulkes, S. H. (1974). My philosophy in psychotherapy. In: S. H. Foulkes, *Selected Papers: Psychoanalysis and Group Analysis* (pp. 271–280). London: Karnac, 1990.

Foulkes, S. H. (1975). The leader in the group. In: S. H. Foulkes, *Selected Papers: Psychoanalysis and Group Analysis* (pp. 285–296). London: Karnac, 1990.

Foulkes, S. H. (2003). Mind. *Group Analysis, 36*: 315–321.

Foulkes, S. H., & Anthony, E. J. (1957). *Group Psychotherapy: The Psychoanalytic Approach.* London: Karnac, 1984.

Freud, S. (1905e). Fragment of an analysis of a case of hysteria. *S. E., 7*: 7–112. London: Hogarth.

Freud, S. (1919h). The "Uncanny". *S. E., 17*: 217–252. London: Hogarth.

Freud, S. (1920a). The psychogenesis of a case of female homosexuality. *S. E., 18*: 145–174.

Freud, S. (1921c). *Group Psychology and the Analysis of the Ego. S. E., 18*: 69–144. London: Hogarth.

Freud, S. (1933a). *New Introductory Lectures on Psycho-Analysis. S. E., 22*: 5–158.

Freud, S. (1937d). Constructions in analysis. *S. E., 23*: 257–269.

Frosh, S. (1997). *For and Against Psychoanalysis.* London: Routledge.

Frosh, S. (2014). The nature of the psychosocial. *Journal of Psycho-Social Studies, 8*: 159–169.

Gallop, J. (1982). *Feminism and Psychoanalysis: The Daughter's Seduction.* London: Macmillan.

Gerald of Wales (1951). *History and Topography of Ireland* (Trans. J. O'Mear). London: Penguin (first published 1188).

Gilbert, G., & Gubar, S. (1979). *The Madwomen in the Attic.* New Haven, CT: Yale University Press.

Giles, H., Coupland, J., & Coupland, N. (1991). *Contexts of Accommodation: Developments in Applied Sociolinguistics.* Cambridge: Cambridge University Press.

Gilmore, D. (1993). *Monsters: Evil Beings, Mythical Beasts and All Manner of Imaginary Terrors.* Philadelphia, PA: University of Pennsylvania Press.

Gilmore, S. (1994). *Autobiographics: A Feminist Theory of Women's Self-Representation.* Ithaca, NY: Cornell University Press.

Goffman, E. (1963). *Stigma: Notes on the Management of Spoiled Identity.* Harmondsworth: Penguin.

Goffman, E. (1981). *Forms of Talk.* Philadelphia, PA: University of Pennsylvania Press.

Goldberg, A. (1990). *The Prison-house of Psychoanalysis.* New Jersey: The Analytic Press.

Grafton, A. (1992). *New Worlds, Ancient Texts.* Cambridge, MA: Harvard University Press.

Guiton, G. (2012). *The Early Quakers and the Kingdom of God: Peace, Testimony and Revolution.* San Francisco, CA: Inner Light.

Habermas, J. (1989). *The Structural Transformation of the Public Sphere* (Trans. T. Burger). Cambridge: Polity.

Hacking, I. (2012). Introduction. In: T. Kuhn, *The Structure of Scientific Revolutions.* Chicago, IL: University of Chicago Press.

Hanafi, Z. (2000). *The Monster in the Machine: Magic, Medicine and the Marvellous in the Time of the Scientific Revolution.* Durham, NC: Duke University Press.

Hänninen, V., & Koski-Jännes, A. (2004). Stories of attempts to recover from addiction. In: P. Rosenqvist, A. Koski-Jännes, & L. Ojesjo (Eds.), *Addiction and the Life Course.* Helsinki: NAD.

Harré, R. (1997). Pathological autobiographies. *Philosophy, Psychiatry and Psychology, 4:* 99–109.

Harré, R. (2010). Individual lives and social trajectories. In: L. Van Langenhove (Ed.), *People and Society: Rom Harré and Designing the Social Sciences.* London: Routledge.

Harré, R., & Van Langenhove, L. (1991). Varieties of positioning. *Journal for the Theory of Social Behaviour, 21:* 393–407.

Harré, R., Moghaddam, F., Pilkerton Cairnie, T., Rothbart, D., & Sabat, S. (2009). Recent advances in positioning theory. *Theory and Psychology, 19:* 5–31.

Hassin, R., Uleman, J., & Bargh, J. (2005). *The New Unconscious.* Oxford: Oxford University Press.

Hearst, L. (1993). Our cultural cargo and its vicissitudes in group analysis. *Group Analysis, 26:* 389–405.

Hekma, G., & Giami, A. (Eds.) (2014). *Sexual Revolutions.* Basingstoke: Palgrave Macmillan.

Herlihy, D. (1997). *The Black Death and the Transformation of the West.* Cambridge, MA: Harvard University Press.

Hermans, H. (2001). The dialogical self: towards a theory of personal and cultural positioning. *Culture and Psychology, 7:* 243–281.

Hermans, H. (2003). The construction and reconstruction of a dialogical self. *Journal of Constructivist Psychology, 16:* 89–130.

Hermans, H. (2004). The dialogical self: between exchange and power. In: H. Hermans & G. Dimaggio (Eds.), *The Dialogical Self in Psychotherapy*. New York: Brunner Routledge.

Hermans, H. (2006). The self as a theatre of voices. *Journal of Constructivist Psychology, 19*: 147–169.

Hermans, H., & Dimaggio, G. (Eds.) (2004a). *The Dialogical Self in Psychotherapy*. New York: Brunner-Routledge.

Hermans, H., & Dimaggio, G. (2004b). Introduction: The dialogical self in psychotherapy. In: H. Hermans & G. Dimaggio (Eds.), *The Dialogical Self in Psychotherapy*. New York: Brunner-Routledge.

Hermans, H., & Hermans-Konopka, A. (2010). *Dialogical Self Theory: Positioning and Counter-Positioning in a Globalizing Society*. Cambridge: Cambridge University Press.

Higgs Strickland, D. (2000). Monsters and Christian enemies. *History Today, 50*: 45–51.

Higgs Strickland, D. (2010). The future is necessarily monstrous. *Different Visions: A Journal of new Perspectives on Medieval Art, 2*: 1–13.

Higgs Strickland, D. (2012). Monstrosity and race in the late Middles Ages. In: A. Mittman & P. Dendle (Eds.), *The Ashgate Research Companion to Monsters and the Monstrous* (Chapter Seventeen). Farnham: Ashgate.

Hill, C. (1972). *The World Turned Upside Down: Radical Ideas During the English Revolution*. London: Penguin.

Hill, C. (1990). *A Nation of Change and Novelty: Radical Politics, Religions and Literature in 17th-Century England*. London: Routledge & Kegan Paul.

Hinshelwood, R. (1995). Psychoanalysis in Britain: points of cultural access, 1893–1918. *International Journal of Psychoanalysis, 76*: 135–149.

Hobsbawm, E. (1969). *Bandits*. London: Weidenfeld & Nicolson.

Hobsbawm, E. (1977). *On History*. London: Weidenfeld & Nicolson.

Holloway, W. (1984). Gender difference and the production of subjectivity. In: J. Henriques, W. Hollway, C Venn, & V. Walkerdine (Eds.), *Changing the Subject*. London: Methuen.

Hopper, E. (1991). Encapsulation as a defence against the fear of annihilation. *International Journal of Psychoanalysis, 72*: 607–624.

Hsia, R. po-Chia (2004). A time for monsters. In: L. Knoppers & J. Landes (Eds.), *Monstrous Bodies/Political Monstrosities in Early Modern Europe*. Ithaca, NY: Cornell University Press.

Hulme, P. (1984). Polytropic man: tropes of sexuality and mobility in early colonial discourse. In: F. Barker, P. Hulme, M. Iveson, & D. Loxley (Eds.), *Europe and its Others, Vol. 2*. Colchester: University of Essex.

Hulme, P. (1986). *Colonial Encounters: Europe and the Native Caribbean 1492–1797*. London: Methuen.

Humphreys, K. (2000). Community narratives and personal stories in Alcoholics Anonymous. *Journal of Community Psychology*, 28: 495–506.

Hunt, L. (1983). Hercules and the radical image in the French Revolution. *Representations*, 2: 95–117.

Hunt, L. (1990). Discourses of patriarchism and anti-patricarchism in the French Revolution. In: J. Renwick (Ed.), *Language and Rhetoric of the Revolution*. Edinburgh: Edinburgh University Press.

Inwood, M. (1997). *A Very Short Introduction to Heidegger*. Oxford: Blackwell.

Jacobs, D. (1996). Voice. In: *Encyclopaedia of Rhetoric and Composition* T. Enos (Ed.) (pp. 740- 753). London: Taylor & Francis.

Jones, M. (1958). *The Therapeutic Community: A New Treatment Method in Psychiatry*. New York: Basic.

Jung, C. G. (1967). Letter from Carl Jung. In: Bill W., *As Bill Sees It*. Alcoholics Anonymous.

Khantzian, E. (1995). Alcoholics Anonymous: cult or corrective. *Journal of Substance Abuse Treatment*, 12: 157–165.

Khantzian, E., & Mack, J. (1989). Alcoholics Anonymous and contemporary psychodynamic theory. In: M. Galanter (Ed.), *Alcoholism*, Vol. 7. New York: Plenum.

Khayyám, O. (1992). *Rubáiyát of Omar Khayyám* (Trans. E. Fitzgerald). Boston, MA: Branden.

Kiryanova, E. (2015). Images of kingship: Charles I, accession ceremony and the theory of Divine Right. *History*, 100: 21–39.

Knox, J. (2013). The analytic institute as a psychic retreat: Why we need to include research evidence in our clinical training. *British Journal of Psychotherapy*, 29, 424–448.

Kohut, H. (1981). Idealisation and cultural selfobjects. In: C. Strozier (Ed.), *Self Psychology and the Humanities*. New York: W.W. Norton.

Koski-Jännes, A. (2002). Social and personal identity projects in the recovery from addictive behaviours. *Addiction Research and Theory*, 10: 183–202.

Kruger, S. (2005). *The Spectral Jew: Conversion and Embodiment in Medieval Europe*. Minneapolis, MN: University of Minnesota Press.

Kuhn, T. S. (1962). *The Structure of Scientific Revolutions*. Chicago, IL: University of Chicago Press, 2012.

Kuhn, T. S. (1977). *The Essential Tension*. Chicago, IL: The University of Chicago Press.

Kurtz, E. (1982). Why AA Works; the intellectual significance of Alcoholics Anonymous. *Journal of Studies in Alcohol*, 43: 38–80.

Laclau, E. (1996). *Emancipation(s)*. London: Verso.

Lakoff, G., & Johnson, M. (1980). *Metaphors We Live By*. Chicago, IL: University of Chicago Press.

Landes, J. (2004). Revolutionary anatomies. In: L. Knoppers & J. Landes (Eds.), *Monstrous Bodies/Political Monstrosities in Early Modern Europe* (Chapter Six). Ithaca, NY: Cornell University Press.

Langmuir, G. (1990). *Toward a Definition of Anti-Semitism.* Berkeley, CA: University of California Press.

Laplanche, J., & Leclaire, S. (1972). The unconscious: a psychoanalytic study. *Yale French Studies, 48*: 118–178.

Larner, C. (1984). *Witchcraft and Religion: The Politics of Popular Belief.* London: Blackwell.

Leach, E. (1982). Anthropological aspects of language: animal categories and verbal abuse. In: W. Lessa & E. Vogt (Eds.), *Reader in Comparative Religion.* New York: Harper & Row.

Lefebvre, H. (1991). *The Production of Space* (Trans. D. Nicholson-Smith). Oxford: Blackwell.

Lemaire, A. (1979). *Jacques Lacan.* Hove: Routledge.

Lesser, R., & Schoenberg, E. (Eds.) (1999). *That Obscure Object of Desire: Freud's Female Homosexual Patient Revisited.* New York: Routledge.

Levine, H. (1978). The discovery of addiction: changing conceptions of habitual drunkenness in America. *Journal of Studies on Alcohol, 39*: 143–173.

Lewin, K. (1951). *Field Theory in Social Science: Selected Theoretical Papers* (Ed., D. Cartwright). New York: Harper & Row.

Lewis, B. (2012). Recovery, narrative theory and generative madness. In: A. Rudnick (Ed.), *Recovery for People with Mental Illness: Philosophical and Related Perspectives* (Chapter Ten). Oxford: Oxford University Press.

Lichtenberg, J., Lachmann, F., & Fossage, J. (2002). *A Spirit of Inquiry: Communication in Psychoanalysis.* Hilsdale, NJ: The Analytic Press.

Liston, K. (2012). Editor's introduction: long-term perspectives on the human condition. *Human Figurations, 1/1.*

Locke, J. (1689/2009). *Of the Abuse of Words.* London: Penguin.

Long Hoeveler, D. (2004). *Frankenstein,* feminism and literary theory. In: E. Schor (Ed.), *The Cambridge Companion to Mary Shelley* (Chapter 3). Cambridge: Cambridge University Press.

MacIntyre, A. (1984). *After Virtue: A Study in Moral Theory.* Notre Dame, IN: University of Notre Dame Press.

Mack, J. (1981). Alcoholism, AA and governance of self. In: M. Bean & N. Zinberg (Eds.), *Dynamic Approaches to Understanding and Treatment of Alcoholism.* New York: Free Press.

Main, T. (1989; original lecture, 1981). The concept of the therapeutic community variations and vicissitudes. In: J. John (Ed.), *The Ailment and Other Psychoanalytic Essays.* London: Free Association.

Malchow, H. (1993). Frankenstein's monster and images of race in 19th-century Britain. *Past and Present, 139*: 90–130.

Maraki, G. (2008). *Revolution in Mind: The Creation of Psychoanalysis*. London: Duckworth.

Marcus, S. (1981). Freud and Dora: story, history, case history. In: P. Meisel (Ed.), *Freud: A Collection of Critical Essays*. New Jersey: Prentice-Hall.

Markham, C. R. (Ed.) (2010). *The Journal of Christopher Columbus (During His First Voyage, 1492–93)*. Oxford: OUP.

Marratos, J. (2006). The power of myth as metaphor. *Group Analysis, 39*: 87–99.

Marx, K. (1848). *The Communist Manifesto.*

McAdams, D. (2008). Personal narratives and the life story. In: J. Robins & P. Previn (Eds.), *Handbook of Personality: Theory and Research*. New York: Guildford Press.

McDougall, J. (1977). Interview. In: *Freely Associated*. London: Free Association.

McDougall, J. (1986). *Theatres of the Mind: Illusion and Truth on the Psychoanalytic Stage*. London: Free Association.

McIntosh, J., & McKeganey, N. (2000). Addicts' narratives of recovery from drug use: Constructing a non-addict identity. *Social Science and Medicine, 50*: 1501–1510.

McLeod, S. (2010). *Zone of Proximal Development—Scaffolding—Simply Psychology*. Retrieved from http://www.simplypsychology.org/Zone-of-Proximal-Development.html

Mellor, A. (2003). Making a monster. In: E. Schor (Ed.), *The Cambridge Companion to Mary Shelley* (Chapter One). Cambridge: Cambridge University Press.

Merrick, J. (1998). The body politics of French absolutism. In: S. Melzer & K. Norberg (Eds.), *From the Royal to the Republican Body: Incorporating the Political in Seventeenth- and Eighteenth-Century France*. Berkeley, CA: University of California Press.

Miller, W., & Kurtz, E. (1994). Models of alcoholism used in treatment: contrasting AA and other perspectives with which it is often confused. *Journal of Studies of Alcohol, 55*: 159–166.

Milton, J. (2004). *Paradise Lost* (Eds. S. Orgel & J. Goldberg). Oxford: OUP.

Mitchell, J. (1974). *Psychoanalysis and Feminism*. London: Allen Lane.

Mojovi , M. (2011). Manifestations of psychic retreats in social systems. In: E. Hopper & H. Weinberg (Eds.), *The Social Unconscious in Persons, Groups and Societies, Volume 1*. London: Karnac.

Moore, R. (2014). *The War on Heresy: Faith and Power in Medieval Europe*. London: Profile.

Morrill, J. S. (Ed.) (1991). *The Impact of the Civil War*. London: Collins and Brown.

Moscovici, S. (2007) *Psychoanalysis: Its Image and its Public*. Cambridge: Polity.

Mulkay, M. (1988). *On Humour*. Cambridge: Cambridge University Press.

Murray, R. (1995). Narrative partitioning: the ins and outs of identity construction. In: J. Smith, R. Harre, & L. van Langenhove (Eds.), *Rethinking Psychology: Volume 1- Conceptual Foundations*. London: Sage.

Nietzsche, F. (1872–1873). Ancient rhetoric. In: S. L. Gilman, C. Blair, & D. J. Parent (Eds. & Trans.), *Frederic Nietzsche on Rhetoric and Language*. Oxford: OUP, 1989.

Nirenberg, D. (2013). *Anti-Judaism: The History of a Way of Thinking*. New York: W.W. Norton.

Nitsun, M. (2015). *Beyond the Anti-Group*. London: Routledge.

Norris, C. (1983). *The Deconstructive Turn: Essays in the Rhetoric of Philosophy*. London: Methuen.

Nye, R. (1995). Introduction. In: G. Le Bon, *The Crowd*. New Brunswick, NJ: Transaction.

O'Halloran, S. (2008). *Talking Oneself Sober: The Discourse of Alcoholics Anonymous*. Amherst, NY: Cambria.

Ormay, T. (2012). *The Social Nature of Persons: One Person is no Person*. London: Karnac.

O'Shaughnessy, E. (1992). Enclaves and excursions. *International Journal of Psychoanalysis*, 73: 603–614.

Pagden, A. (1982). *The Fall of Natural Man: The American Indian and the Origins of Comparative Ethnology*. Cambridge: Cambridge University Press.

Pagden, A. (1993). *European Encounters with the New World*. New Haven, CT: Yale University Press.

Perkins, R., & Rinaldi, M. (2007). *Taking Back Control: A Guide to Planning Your Own Recovery*. South West London and St. George's Mental Health NHS Trust.

Phillips, A. (2006). The sweet smell of excess. *Guardian Review* (p. 21), 28 January 2006.

Piaget, J. (1973). The affective unconscious and the cognitive unconscious. *Journal of the American Psychoanalytic Association*, 21: 249–261.

Pines, M. (1988). Psychoanalysis, psychodrama and group psychotherapy. *Group Analysis*, 19: 101–112.

Pines, M. (1991). The matrix of group analysis; a historical perspective. *Group Analysis*, 24: 99–109.

Pines, M. (1998). *Circular Reflections: Selected Papers on Group Analysis and Psychoanalysis*. London: Jessica Kingsley.

Pines, M. (2006). How can group analysis become an academic discipline? *Group Analysis*, 39: 273–280.

Pinker, S. (2007). The evolutionary social psychology of off-record speech acts. *Intercultural Pragmatics*, 4: 437–461.

Rachum, I. (1995). The meaning of "revolution" in the English Revolution (1648–1660). *Journal of the History of Ideas*, 56: 195–215.

Reedy, W. (1994). The historical imaginary of social science in post-revolutionary France. *History of the Human Sciences, 7*: 1–26.

Repper, J., & Perkins, R. (2003). *Social Inclusion and Recovery.* London: Baillière Tindall.

Ricoeur, P. (1992). *Oneself as Another* (Trans. K. Blamey). Chicago, IL: University of Chicago Press.

Roazen, P. (1969). *Brother Animal: The Story of Freud and Tausk.* New York: Knopf.

Robinson, C. (1996). Alcoholics Anonymous as seen from the perspective of self-psychology. *Smith College Studies in Social Work, 66*: 129–145.

Roland, A. (2001). Another voice and position: psychoanalysis across civilisations. *Culture and Psychology, 7*: 311–321.

Rose, J. (1978). Dora: Fragments of an analysis. *M/F, 2*: 5–21.

Rose, J. (1983). Femininity and its discontents. *Feminist Review, 14*: 5–21.

Rose, N. (1990). *Governing the Soul: The Shaping of the Private Self.* London: Routledge.

Rose, N. (1992). Engineering the human soul: analysing psychological expertise. *Science in Context, 5*: 351–369.

Rosenbaum, M. (1975). Introduction: In: S. H. Foulkes, *Group-Analytic Psychotherapy: Method and Practices.* New York: Gordon & Breach.

Roustang, F. (1976). *Dire Mastery: Discipleship from Freud to Lacan.* Washington: American Psychiatric Press.

Roustang, F. (1982). *Psychoanalysis Never Lets Go.* Baltimore, MA: Johns Hopkins University Press.

Rowbotham, S. (1973). *Hidden from History.* London: Pluto.

Rowbotham, S., Segal, L., & Wainwright, H. (1979). *Beyond the Fragments.* London: Merlin.

Rubin, M. (1999). *Gentile Tales: The Narrative Assault on Late Medieval Jews.* New Haven, CT: Yale University Press.

Rudé, G. (1964). *Revolutionary Europe, 1783–1815.* London: Fontana.

Rudé, G. (1995). *The Crowd in History.* London: Serif, 2005.

Rule, A. (2005). Ordered thoughts on thought disorder. *Psychiatric Bulletin, 29*: 462–464.

Rustin, M. (1991). The social organisation of secrets: towards a sociology of psychoanalysis. In: *The Good Society and the Inner World: Psychoanalysis, Politics and Culture.* London: Verso.

Said, E. (1978). *Orientalism.* London: Penguin.

Said, E. (1984). Permission to narrate. *London Review of Books,* February.

Scribner, B. (2002). Preconditions of tolerance and intolerance. In: P. Grell & B. Scribner (Eds.), *Tolerance and Intolerance in the European Reformation.* Cambridge: Cambridge University Press.

Sewell, W. H. (1994). *A Rhetoric of Bourgeois Revolution: Abbé Sieyes and "What is the Third Estate?".* Durham, NC: Duke University Press.

Shakespeare, W. *Richard III.*

Shakespeare, W. *The Tempest.*

Sharpe, K., & Zwicker, S. (Eds.) (1998). *Refiguring Revolutions: Aesthetics and Politics from the English Revolution to the Romantic Revolution.* Berkeley, CA: University of California Press.

Shelley, M. (2012; original publication, 1818). *Frankenstein; or, the Modern Prometheus.* London: Penguin.

Simmel, G. (1971). *On Individuality and Social Forms* (Ed. D. Levine). Chicago, IL: University of Chicago Press.

Smith, R. (1997). *The Fontana History of the Human Sciences.* London: Fontana.

Spence, D. (1982). *Narrative Truth and Historical Truth: Meaning and Interpretation in Psychoanalysis.* New York: Norton.

Spurling, L. (Ed.) (1993). Introduction. In: L. Spurling (Ed.), *From the Words of my Mouth: Tradition in Psychotherapy.* London: Routledge.

St. Augustine (1958). *City of God* (Abridged by V. Bourke). New York: Doubleday (originally published AD 426).

Stacey, R. (2001). What can it mean to say that the individual is social through and through? *Group Analysis, 34*: 457–471.

Stedman Jones, G. (2013). *Outcast London; A Study in the Relationship between Classes in Victorian Society.* London: Verso.

Steiner, J. (1990). *Psychic Retreats: Pathological Organisations in Psychotic, Neurotic and Borderline Patients.* London: Routledge.

Stern, D. B. (1996). The social construction of therapeutic action. *Psychoanalytic Inquiry, 16*: 265–293.

Sterrenburg, L. (1979). Mary Shelley's monster: politics and psyche in Frankenstein. In: G. Levine & U. Knoepflacher (Eds.), *The Endurance of Frankenstein: Essays on Mary Shelley's Novel.* Berkeley, CA: University of California Press.

Stevenson, R. L. (1979). *The Strange case of Dr. Jekyll and Mr. Hyde and Other Stories* (Ed. J. Calder). London: Penguin (first published 1886).

Sulloway, F. (1979). *Freud, Biologist of the Mind: Beyond the Psychoanalytic Legend.* New York: Basic.

Sulloway, F. (1992). Reassessing Freud's case histories. In: T. Gelfand & J. Kerr (Eds.), *Freud and the History of Psychoanalysis.* Hillsdale, NJ: The Analytic Press.

Swora, M. (2001). Commemoration and the healing of memories in Alcoholics Anonymous. *Ethos, 29*: 58–77.

Taylor, C. (1976). Hermeneutics and politics. In: P. Connerton (Ed.), *Critical Sociology: Selected Readings* (Chapter Eight). London: Penguin.

Thompson, E. P. (1980). *The Making of the English Working Class.* Harmondsworth: Penguin.

Thomson, R. G. (1996). *Freakery: Cultural spectacles of the Extraordinary Body.* New York: New York University Press.

Tiebout, H. (1944). Therapeutic mechanisms of Alcoholics Anonymous. *American Journal of Psychiatry, 100*: 488–473.

Todorov, T. (1984). *The Conquest of America*. New York: Harper & Row.

Tully, J. (1988). Governing conduct. In: E. Leites (Ed.), *Conscience and Casuistry in Early Modern Europe*. Cambridge: Cambridge University Press.

Turner, B. (2012). Embodied practice: Martin Heidegger, Pierre Bourdieu, Michel Foucault. In: B. Turner (Ed.), *Routledge Handbook of Body Studies* (Chapter Four). London: Routledge.

Turner, J. C., Hogg, M. A., Oakes, P. J., Reicher, S. D., & Wetherell, M. S. (1987). *Rediscovering the Social Group: A Self-Categorization Theory*. New York: Blackwell.

Turner, M. (1996). *The Literary Mind: The Origins of Thought and Language*. Oxford: Oxford University Press.

Ullman, W. (1972). *Medieval Political Thought*. Middlesex: Penguin.

Van Ginneken, J. (1992). *Crowds, Psychology, and Politics, 1871–1899*. Cambridge: Cambridge University Press.

Wallace, M. (2009). *Revolutionary Subjects in the English "Jacobin" Novel, 1790–1805*. Lewisburg, PA: Bucknell University Press.

Walsh, J. (2006). The intermediate space: the border country. *Group Analysis, 39*: 185–197.

Weber, S. (1982). *The Legend of Freud*. Minneapolis, MN: University of Minnesota Press.

Weegmann, M. (2004). Alcoholics Anonymous: a group-analytic view of fellowship organisations. *Group Analysis, 37*: 243–258.

Weegmann, M. (2005a). Dangerous cocktails: drugs and alcohol in the family. In: M. Boyer (Ed.), *Psychoanalytic Theory for Social Work Practice: Thinking Under Fire*. London: Routledge.

Weegmann, M. (2005b). "If each could be housed in separate personalities …": therapy as conversation between different parts of the self. *Psychoanalytic Psychotherapy, 19*: 279–293.

Weegmann, M. (2008). Monsters: the social-unconscious life of "Others" and a note on the origins of group theory. *Group Analysis, 41*: 291–300.

Weegmann, M. (2011). Psychodynamics in groups or psychodynamic groups? In: R. Hill & J. Harris (Eds.), *Principles and Practices of Group Work in Addictions*. London: Routledge.

Weegmann, M. (2014a). *The World Within the Group: Developing Theory for Group Analysis*. London: Karnac.

Weegmann, M. (2014b). Reforming subjectivity: personal, familial and group implications of the English Reformation. In: *The World Within the Group: Developing Theory for Group Analysis*. London: Karnac.

Weegmann, M., & English, C. (2010). Beyond the shadow of drugs; groups with substance misusers. *Group Analysis, 43*: 3–21.

Weegmann, M., & Piwowoz-Hjort, E. (2009). "Naught but a story": narratives of successful AA recovery. *Health Sociology Review, 18*: 273–283.

White, H. (1972). Forms of wildness; archaeology of an idea. In: E. Dudley & D. Lovak (Eds.), *The Wild Man Within: An Image in Western Thought from the Renaissance to Romanticism* (Chapter Four). Pittsburgh, PA: University of Pittsburgh Press.

White, M. (2004). Folk psychology and narrative practice. In: L. E. Angus & J. McLeod (Eds.), *The Handbook of Narrative Psychotherapy: Practice, Theory and Research* (Chapter Two). London: Sage.

White, W., Laudet, A. B., & Becker, J. B. (2006). Life meaning and purpose in addiction recovery. *Addiction Professional, 4*: 18–23.

Williams, D. (1999). *Deformed Discourse: The Function of the Monster in Mediaeval Thought and Literature*. Montreal: McGill-Queen's University Press.

Wind, B. (1998). *A Foul and Pestilent Congregation: Images of "Freaks" in Baroque Art*. Aldershot: Ashgate.

Winnicott, D. W. (1962). The theory of the parent-infant relationship: further remarks. *International Journal of Psychoanalysis, 43*: 238–239.

Wittkower, R. (1942). Marvels of the East: a study in the history of monsters. *Journal of the Warburg and Courtauld Institutes, 5*: 159–197.

Wollstonecraft, M. (2004). *A Vindication of the Rights of Women*. London: Penguin.

Woolf, L. (1981). Everyday life. In: P. Meisel (Ed.), *Freud: A Collection of Critical Essays*. Engelwood Cliffs, NJ: Prentice-Hall.

Wyse, H. (1996). Was Wittgenstein a group analyst? *Group Analysis, 29*: 355–368.

Yalom, I. (1983). *Inpatient Group Psychotherapy*. New York: Basic.

Yorke, L. (1997). *Adrienne Rich: Passion, Politics and the Body*. London: Sage.

INDEX

139

142   INDEX